THE POWER OF INTERMITTENT FASTING FOR WOMEN OVER 50

REIGNITE ENERGY, BALANCE HORMONES, BURN FAT, AND BOOST MENTAL CLARITY FOR A VIBRANT, YOUTHFUL LIFE

CLAUDIA VON

INTRODUCTION

As I approached my 50th birthday, I began to feel the effects of aging. I had less energy, gained weight, and felt like I was losing the mental clarity I once had. I was determined to fight the aging process at every step. As such, I am always looking for ways to look and feel my best. I discovered Intermittent fasting through my cardiologist, who also specializes in the field of longevity. He has authored several books on heart-healthy diets but has recently been focusing on intermittent fasting due to its effects on longevity. I had heard some ladies at the gym discussing intermittent fasting, so I asked him about it at my last appointment. Our discussion piqued my curiosity, and I decided to do more research. What I found and learned was nothing less than life-changing.

Like many who have heard of intermittent fasting and its benefits, I was initially skeptical. Could changing my eating schedule possibly have such a significant impact? Yet, the more research I did, the more I understood the science and the tremendous impact it could have on my overall health. I knew I had to try it. I started small, making subtle changes to my life, and was amazed at the outcome. Those stubborn extra pounds I had been carrying around finally began to disappear. I also experienced a significant increase in energy and mental clarity. I am just at the beginning of my fasting journey, but my excitement is not containable. Compared to other longevity solutions I have tried, this lifestyle change is all-natural, inexpensive, and accessible to everyone. And the results are simply amazing!

This book is the result of my passion for sharing this excellent tool with other women over 50 who, like me, are seeking natural and effective ways to enhance their health and well-being. If you're facing hormonal imbalances, trying to manage your weight, or experiencing cognitive decline, intermittent fasting could be an excellent option for you.

What This Book Is About

This book delves into the benefits of intermittent fasting in detail, demystifying the science and highlighting its specific advantages for women over 50. However, far from being just a hypothetical manual, the book is packed with practical advice, meal ideas, recipes, and exercise tips, offering a seamless approach to incorporating intermittent fasting into your routine.

I know that adopting a new way of living can be daunting, especially after decades of adhering to established customs and rituals. That is where I come in to guide the transition and provide information about intermittent fasting that is easy to understand and highly engaging.

Inside this guide, you'll learn how to:

1. Choose a fasting schedule that effortlessly incorporates into your routine.
2. Maximize your nutrient consumption at mealtime.
3. Navigate the holiday and social scenes without sacrificing your objectives.

4. Get customized advice for overcoming common pitfalls and staying motivated throughout the process.
5. Actionable ways to incorporate exercise and mindfulness to maximize your benefits.
6. A holistic approach to easily incorporating intermittent fasting into your life to maximize your results.

Plus, I have included BONUS content at the end of the book that contains recipes specific to digestion and bone health, a weekly meal planning guide, weekly exercise programs, a self-assessment questionnaire to help you determine your fasting schedule, and much more!

All I ask is for you to hold the conviction that, regardless of age or the point at which you start, you carry the power to regain control of your health and redesign your life. What you are doing with intermittent fasting is not just changing the way you eat; you are investing heavily in your health, enhancing both your mind and body.

Whether you're a beginner to intermittent fasting or have some experience, I welcome you to join me on this fascinating path of discovery and empowerment. Let us uncover the secrets of aging gracefully, feeling wonderful, and loving life together.

Let's get started!

1

UNDERSTANDING THE BASICS OF INTERMITTENT FASTING

L ast year, I hit a turning point. Like many women over 50, I was facing changes in my body, including a slower metabolism, weight gain, and a noticeable decline in energy. I was looking for a natural way to combat the aging process, so I decided to give Intermittent Fasting a try. I gradually implemented some of the strategies I learned from my doctor and through my research, and what I discovered was truly transformative.

WHAT IS INTERMITTENT FASTING? A BEGINNER'S GUIDE

Many people think Intermittent Fasting is simply a diet. Although it offers the benefit of weight loss, it also provides numerous other benefits that are even more exciting. Intermittent fasting is an eating pattern that doesn't dictate what to eat but rather when to eat. It cycles between eating periods and fasting periods. Focusing primarily on *when* you eat rather than *what* you eat. At its core, intermittent fasting is a strategic pause in eating that gives your body time to rest, repair, and rebalance.

Intermittent Fasting does not limit what you eat or how much you eat. No more counting calories or food restrictions. It allows you to enjoy your favorite foods within your eating window. It's not about deprivation but about creating a healthy and balanced lifestyle. We often refer to the eating periods as "eating windows" and non-eating periods as "fasting windows." You enjoy all your meals during your eating window. During your fasting window, you eat very little, allowing your body to rest from eating food. What makes it so accessible to everyone is its adaptable approach that integrates into your lifestyle and complements your interests, rather than being restrictive and burdensome. By simply adjusting your eating time, you can achieve a wide range of essential benefits designed for women like us at this stage of our lives.

During fasting, your body undergoes a powerful internal shift. Without incoming food to burn, it begins to use stored fat as fuel, tapping into energy reserves and supporting natural weight loss. At the same time, growth hormone levels increase, which helps preserve lean muscle and accelerate fat metabolism. Behind the scenes, your cells begin deep repair work through a process called autophagy, where they clear out damaged components and regenerate for better function. Insulin levels also drop, improving insulin sensitivity and reducing fat storage, inflammation, and the risk of chronic disease. These combined effects make fasting a reset for both body and mind.

It's not uncommon to hear misconceptions about fasting. Some might worry that it's just another form of starvation or that it's solely about losing weight. Fasting is a principle of balance, not of deprivation. Although weight loss is undoubtedly a welcome side effect, the broader benefits of fasting, such as improved mental clarity, enhanced cognitive function, and increased energy, are even more impactful on your overall health. It works in perfect synchrony with the body's processes, enhancing cellular cleansing and detoxification.

For those new to fasting, the idea of going hours without food might seem unrealistic. This is where the flexibility of Intermittent Fasting is a game-changer. You can choose a schedule that suits your lifestyle, and adjust it as needed. Beginners should starting gradually with a 12-hour fast, which is as easy as eating dinner at 7 p.m. and breakfast at 7 a.m. As fasting becomes more habitual, you can gradually increase the time in small increments until you achieve your goals.

Remember, the idea is to find a method that you identify with, something that is free from pressure and stress. Intermittent fasting is all about balance and harmony, allowing you to connect with the natural rhythms of your body. As you venture forth into this new path, keep in mind that you're not alone. In the following chapters, we will delve into how this simple yet powerful practice can transform your health and overall well-being.

FASTING PROTOCOLS: FINDING YOUR PERFECT TIMING

When starting intermittent fasting, you have several fasting schedules to choose from, each suited to various lifestyles and needs.

The most frequently used **16:8** plan consists of a 16-hour fasting period and an 8-hour eating period. The flexibility of this approach allows your meals to integrate into your daily lifestyle easily. For example, if you eat breakfast at 10 a.m., aim to finish dinner by 6 p.m. or adjust the time to fit your schedule. This method is most effective for weight loss, as it naturally reduces daily calorie intake, supports fat burning without requiring severe calorie counting, and is sustainable in the long term for most people.

The **14:10** or **12:12** methods involve a 14 or 12-hour fasting interval with a 10 or 12-hour eating period. This schedule is most suitable for beginners, as it allows for longer eating windows and more flexibility, avoiding the challenge of feeling hungry. Its built-in adaptability achieves a healthy equilibrium in hormone levels. It is equally effective in promoting energy, maintaining a stable weight, and reducing symptoms of menopause.

The **5:2** method involves eating normally for five days and reducing calories significantly (around 500-600 calories) for the remaining two non-consecutive days. The technique is ideal for individuals who enjoy a fixed fasting routine. This approach enhances metabolic health by improving insulin sensitivity, reducing inflammation, and encouraging metabolic flexibility (burning fat and sugar efficiently).

The fourth option is the **alternate-day** approach. It is the most extreme option. On this schedule, you fast every other day. You aim to eat less than 500 calories on both days you fast. You can eat normally without restrictions, but only healthy foods are allowed. It is best suited for those who are advanced in intermittent fasting, prefer a more rigid timetable, and wish to reap the maximum benefits from fasting, such as effective, rapid weight loss, substantial improvements in insulin sensitivity and blood sugar regulation, significant cellular repair (autophagy), and fat burning. All the while preserving muscle mass, as long as you include enough protein in your diet on your eating days.

HOW INTERMITTENT FASTING DIFFERS FOR WOMEN OVER 50

When considering a lifestyle change like intermittent fasting, especially in our 50s, it is crucial to pay close attention to hormonal changes, bone health, nutritional needs, inflammation, insulin resistance, and cognitive function.

Hormonal imbalances, particularly during perimenopause and menopause, affect everything from mood to weight. Since fasting can be a stressor, it is essential to start slowly and select a gentle fasting schedule. Menopause also increases the risk of insulin resistance and chronic inflammation. However, intermittent fasting creates a more even hormonal state that may reduce some menopause symptoms, such as hot flashes, mood swings, and sleep deprivation. When paired with an anti-inflammatory diet, you may experience a reduction in inflammation.

As we turn 50, our nutritional needs begin to change. Our bones, in particular, require a little more care. Calcium and Vitamin D are our protective guardians when it comes to maintaining healthy bones and preventing osteoporosis. Leafy vegetables, whole grains, and fatty fish, such as salmon, should be part of our diet now. Additionally, a planned intake of protein helps maintain our muscle mass, which tends to decline with age. With a planned intake of protein in the form of meat plus milk, we can protect our muscles, and this, in turn, contributes to a healthier, stronger body.

As we age, clarity of mind can sometimes seem elusive. Intermittent fasting can help cognitive health by boosting the brain-derived neurotrophic factor (BDNF). **BDNF** is a protein that helps grow new neurons and strengthens existing brain pathways. It also triggers autophagy, encouraging a sharp mind. This leads to better memory, sharper focus, and faster learning.

SCIENCE OF FASTING: HORMONE BALANCE AND METABOLISM

Intermittent fasting is a powerful catalyst for profound health changes, particularly during the complex changes that characterize menopause. As the hormonal balance during this time of a woman's life seems tenuous at best, affecting not only her emotions but even her bodily metabolic processes, one of the things that is truly remarkable about intermittent fasting is the way that it increases insulin sensitivity. As we age, our bodies become less responsive to insulin. This hormone regulates insulin levels, which can contribute to weight gain and an increased risk of type 2 diabetes. Intermittent fasting can improve insulin sensitivity, making your body more effective at regulating blood sugar levels and reducing the risk of insulin resistance. This can be of enormous assistance to menopausal women, as hormonal changes fuel these issues.

Another significant benefit of fasting is its stabilizing effect on estrogen levels. Not only does estrogen become imbalanced, but it also declines as menopause unfolds, bringing with it a multitude of accompanying discomforts in the form of hot flashes and mood swings. Intermittent fasting naturally aligns with the body's rhythms, stabilizing estrogen levels and providing relief from many uncomfortable symptoms. Fasting also boosts adrenal function, providing an added benefit. The adrenal glands play a crucial role in regulating the stress hormone cortisol. By giving your body periodic breaks from food, fasting reduces the stress on the adrenals, creating a general state of hormonal balance.

Unlocking Metabolic Flexibility Through Fasting

The metabolic benefits of fasting are genuinely remarkable. As we age, our metabolism slows, and we easily accumulate pounds, making their removal a much more formidable feat, turning what had initially been a routine task into what seems like an insurmountable impossibility. Slowly, this change leads to a constant accumulation of weight, primarily in the midsection, as our bodies struggle to burn calories with the same ease that they once had. Fasting paves the way for the acquisition of metabolic flexibility, a remarkable human capacity to transition from carbohydrate to fat utilization as fuel with ease. **Metabolic flexibility** is defined as the body's ability to efficiently switch between using glucose (carbohydrate) and fat as fuel. This flexibility is among the hallmarks of metabolic health. It provides consistent energy, improved blood sugar regulation, stamina, and easier weight control. Conversely, low metabolic flexibility, a characteristic associated with insulin resistance and obesity, can contribute to fatigue, cravings, and a failure to lose weight. Intermittent fasting and exercise are perhaps two of the most effective methods for improving metabolic flexibility.

Metabolic flexibility not only aids in shedding pounds but also helps prevent the accumulation of excess fat. While in a fast, the body relies on stored fat as a source of energy, activating the fat-burning pathway for effective weight management. This technique can be particularly beneficial for women over 50 years old who remain stuck with stubborn weight despite adhering to a healthy diet regimen and a strict workout schedule.

Autophagy: Fasting's Cellular Deep Clean for Healthy Aging

Intermittent Fasting triggers **Autophagy**, a remarkable process in which damaged cellular components are dismantled and recycled, suggesting that fasting can play a crucial role in promoting the development of healthy, resilient cells. This essential process is beneficial for promoting overall health, preventing age-related illnesses, and nurturing health. Researchers have discovered that, aside from promoting longevity, the process is also responsible for preserving mental acuity. Hence, the process emerges as a beneficial way to maintain the health and activity of older adults. Nutritionalists and Endocrinologists have often advocated for the use of partial fasting as a good way to protect physical and mental health.

Inside our cells, Autophagy acts as a deep clean, removing damaged material and paving the way for new, healthy material. This is a natural process where the body cleans out damaged cells and regenerates new ones. This is crucial for healthy aging, immune function, and potentially lowering the risk of age-related diseases like Alzheimer's and cancer. Understanding these concepts will help solidify your understanding of the science behind intermittent fasting and its potential benefits for overall health.

REFLECTIVE EXERCISE: UNDERSTANDING YOUR BODY'S SIGNALS

Let's pause for a moment to observe how your body is feeling. Try to determine when your energy levels are at their peak and when they are at their lowest. Consider how your hunger and mood fluctuate. Write these observations down in a weekly diary. Recording this information will help you identify your body's natural rhythms and learn to integrate the practice of intermittent fasting into your lifestyle. Paying attention to the signs your body gives you will enable you to enjoy the effects of fasting on your hormones and metabolism.

DEBUNKING MYTHS: SEPARATING FACTS FROM FICTION

As we enter the realm of intermittent fasting, it's important to dispel some commonly held myths that might deter you from embracing this beneficial lifestyle.

Muscle Myths Busted: Why Fasting Won't Shrink Your Strength

One of the most frequently voiced concerns is the fear of muscle loss. The idea that fasting will cause your hard-earned muscle mass to reduce is a misconception that needs to be dispelled. This is untrue when done with the right approach. Studies have shown that your muscles are well-preserved when you receive sufficient nutrition within your eating windows. By following a high-protein, nutrient-rich diet, your body can maintain muscle mass while also reaping the additional therapeutic benefits of fasting. This is a common myth that relies on the misconception that food deprivation automatically leads to muscle loss, despite research contradicting this notion. Your body can cope with short fasting periods and, with nutritional provision, can preserve muscle integrity.

Nutrition Myths Busted: Why Fasting Won't Leave You Deficient

Another common misconception is that fasting results in nutritional deficiencies. This seems reasonable since fasting involves skipping food for a specific period. However, the myth cannot hold up when you employ quality, thoughtful fasting practices. The answer lies in what you eat. It is a dedication to consuming a balanced diet full of nutrient-dense foods that enables you to obtain all the nutrition your body needs without a problem. Most of your diet should consist of whole grains, lean protein, and foods rich in vegetables and fruits. These provide the vitamins and minerals your body requires to be at its optimum level. Fasting also enhances your body's ability to absorb and utilize nutrients, so the effect is more one of balancing nutritional intake than a decrease.

Hunger Myths Busted: Why Fasting Doesn't Mean Going Hungry

The idea of going hours without food might seem daunting. Most people find that hunger comes in **waves** and often passes quickly with water, herbal tea, or gentle distraction like walking or journaling. Staying well-hydrated, eating **nutrient-dense meals** during your eating window, and choosing a flexible schedule that suits your lifestyle can make hunger feel more manageable. Over time, your body adapts, and what once felt uncomfortable becomes a sign of healing and self-control.

Energy Myths Busted: Why Fasting Can Boost Your Vitality

You might fear that fasting may leave you feeling weak and depleted, but the opposite is actually true. Done correctly, fasting can enhance energy and mental sharpness. As the body adapts during periods of fasting, it begins using stored fat as fuel, delivering a smooth and steady trickle of energy instead of the high and lows of constant grazing or high-sugar consumption. When you balance your cycle of fasting with rock-solid, nutritious eating during periods of consumption, the lean protein-dense offerings, healthy fats, and a rainbow of bright colors of fruit and vegetable consumption, your blood sugar highs and lows smooth out and give sustained energy all day long. With time and repetition, you may find that you are lighter on your feet, more active, and more energized, in contrast with feeling sluggish and depleted.

Beyond the Fast: Integrating Nutrition, Movement, and Mindfulness for Lasting Health

Fasting should be considered part of a comprehensive approach to a healthy overall lifestyle rather than a temporary solution for weight loss or addressing specific health issues. It is just a part of a larger picture, including synergistic combinations of eating, daily physical training, and mindfulness. Combined synergistically, they work together to create a healthy and active lifestyle. Meals are the perfect time to fuel the system with nutrient-dense, nutritious foods. Physical activity, combined with your eating period, allows you to maximize the impact of Intermittent fasting. Regardless of whether you use weights, walk, or practice yoga, exercise plays a key role in enhancing physical well-being and boosting mood. Mindfulness practices, such as meditation, can help you become even more concentrated and grounded in your fasting regimen.

2

HORMONAL HEALTH AND INTERMITTENT FASTING

D uring the summer months, my husband and I often wake up early to sip our tea and enjoy the stillness of the lake before the weekend warriors arrive. At dawn, the lake is covered in a mist that slowly lifts as the sun rises, revealing clear waters. This image depicts the changes in hormonal balance during menopause, where clarity can emerge from what initially seems turbulent. For many women over 50, menopause begins a new chapter marked by changes that can feel both unfamiliar and unwelcome. The decline in estrogen and progesterone during this time can significantly impact your body, influencing everything from metabolism to weight distribution. As these hormones decrease, they can lead to increased abdominal fat, a slowed metabolism, and a range of daily symptoms. To deal with these changes, we must first understand them.

NAVIGATING MENOPAUSE: FASTING FOR HORMONAL HARMONY

Menopause and perimenopause represent a time when our bodies experience a sophisticated ballet of hormonal ups and downs. Intermittent fasting is a beneficial technique that effectively regulates insulin levels, reduces the impact of inflammation, and promotes smooth coordination among key hormones, such as estrogen and progesterone. It offers an effective strategy for managing hormonal fluctuations in the body, including mood swings and hot flashes. It also helps maintain steady insulin and glucose levels by providing regular breaks for your digestive system, which helps regulate blood sugar levels. Thus lowering your risk of developing insulin resistance, which is prevalent during menopause. Ultimately, intermittent fasting enables your body to adapt more effectively to hormonal changes. Reducing weight gain and energy fluctuations allows your body to tap into its stored fat reserves for energy. Promoting weight management alongside improved metabolic health without forcing restrictive meal plans.

MANAGING HOT FLASHES AND MOOD SWINGS WITH FASTING

Hot flashes and mood swings are two of the most common symptoms of perimenopause and menopause.

Hot flashes arrive unexpectedly and at the most inconvenient times. You get this wave of heat that just sweeps over you like wildfire. Your face gets red, and you feel hot and sweaty instantly, making you look and feel uncomfortable. A hot flash may strike at any time, particularly after experiencing stress, consuming spicy food, or being in a hot environment. Hot flashes disrupt sleep patterns and cause embarrassment. They're a reminder of all the hormonal shifts that have been happening in your body.

Mood swings during menopause make you feel as though you are on an emotional rollercoaster. Your emotions can shift dramatically from peaceful to irritable or sad with no apparent cause. Extreme emotional shifts can lead to overwhelming exhaustion, which can damage interpersonal relationships and disrupt daily functioning.

The symptoms of menopause respond favorably to intermittent fasting as a form of treatment. Fasting enables body temperature regulation by shifting the body into a lower metabolic state during fasting periods, helping the body conserve energy. This can result in a slightly reduced body temperature during the fasting window and may lead to fewer and less severe hot flashes. Fasting also lowers insulin and improves leptin sensitivity. Leptin, made by fat cells, influences metabolism and temperature. When leptin sensitivity improves, the body is better able to maintain temperature homeostasis.

Scientific studies have shown that fasting regulates the endocrine system, leading to improved hormone balance and a reduction in typical menopausal symptoms. The stability of insulin levels achieved during fasting supports hormonal health. It improves emotional control, which in turn enhances mood stability. When you give your body time to rest from digestion and nutrient processing, it can concentrate on maintaining equilibrium, leading to fewer hot flashes and reduced emotional spikes.

Timing is essential for effectively using fasting to alleviate symptoms. A good time to begin fasting is directly after your evening meal. Starting your fasting period after the last evening meal creates a positive atmosphere for the night. This approach reduces discomfort since hot flashes mostly occur during nighttime hours.

The addition of calming activities such as meditation and gentle yoga practice will make your fasting experience more enjoyable. Learn relaxing techniques to minimize stress will aid in managing hot flashes and mood swings. You can use breathing exercises to find your center point and lower stress levels, as stress triggers hot flashes and mood swings.

REFLECTION EXERCISE: UNDERSTANDING YOUR MENOPAUSAL SYMPTOMS

Begin writing in a journal to track your symptoms. Keeping a journal allows you to identify any changes in mood, energy levels, weight, or specific triggers within your body. Tracking your symptoms through journaling will enable you to optimize your fasting schedule and life habits according to your personal needs. Finding your optimal fasting approach will allow you to take control of your health and make intermittent fasting a personalized wellness system.

ENHANCING THYROID HEALTH: FASTING FOR HORMONAL STABILITY

The thyroid gland may be small, but it plays a crucial role in regulating our hormones, particularly as we age. Did you know that your Thyroid gland is located in your neck and shaped like a butterfly? This vital gland produces hormones like thyroxine (T4) and triiodothyronine (T3). Thyroxine (T4) is a key regulator of metabolism. It helps control how your body uses energy and affects body temperature, heart rate, and even brain function. It circulates in the bloodstream and is later converted into a more active hormone called triiodothyronine (T3), directly influencing how your cells produce energy. These hormones play a crucial role in regulating how your body utilizes energy, affecting your mood, and controlling your metabolism. For women over 50, the thyroid plays an even more critical role as it works alongside the hormonal changes that come with menopause. When estrogen and progesterone levels fluctuate, they can impact how the thyroid functions. This might cause some people to feel tired, gain weight, or experience mood swings. Understanding how the thyroid functions can help us comprehend how intermittent fasting enhances performance and maintains hormonal balance.

One of the fantastic perks of fasting is that it helps your body become more sensitive to thyroid hormones. When we give our bodies a break from digesting food, fasting can help our cells function more effectively with thyroid hormones. This enhanced sensitivity may offer a vital tool in our arsenal, enabling us to regulate our food intake and heat production with even greater precision. Furthermore, this will contribute to reducing inflammation and altering thyroid function. Chronic inflammation is something many people deal with, and it can make thyroid problems worse. Reducing inflammation will make our body a more comfortable place for the thyroid gland. When you fast, your body gets busy with processes that help repair cells and remove toxins. This can help reduce some of the stress on your thyroid.

When it comes to maintaining your thyroid health during fasting, several essential considerations are crucial to keep in mind. Monitoring your thyroid levels is vital, especially if you already have a thyroid condition. This helps ensure that any changes you make to your fasting routine won't hurt your thyroid function. Adjusting your fasting schedule to fit your thyroid needs is crucial. For example, some people may prefer longer fasting periods.

In contrast, others may prefer shorter ones that fit better with their lifestyle. Follow the expert guidance from your healthcare provider to make the most informed decision for your unique situation. This may include regular blood tests to check your thyroid hormone levels and help you adjust your fasting plan.

Your nutrient intake is crucial for maintaining optimal thyroid function. A diet packed with selenium, iodine, and zinc can boost your thyroid health, as these nutrients play a key role in hormone production and activity. Seafood, nuts, and whole grains are fantastic options for getting these nutrients. To fast safely, ensure you're getting enough calories and nutrients during your eating windows to maintain your health. This balanced approach is crucial in preventing nutritional deficiencies that can negatively impact your thyroid health. Understanding the relationship between nutrients and your thyroid can help tailor your fasting regimen to promote hormonal equilibrium and enhance your overall health.

SUPPORTING ADRENAL FUNCTION: STRESS MANAGEMENT AND FASTING

Your body's stress response and energy regulation functions heavily depend on the adrenal glands, which reside above your kidneys. The adrenal glands generate cortisol and adrenaline hormones, which help manage stress while maintaining energy stability. The stress hormone cortisol enables your body to handle daily pressures by regulating metabolism, immune function, and blood pressure. The body releases adrenaline during fight-or-flight responses to deliver immediate energy. When stress occurs, it triggers excessive hormone production, resulting in fatigue and overwhelming feelings that resemble a constant alarm in the body. This persistent condition creates adverse effects on your entire body's health.

Intermittent fasting offers a beneficial approach to supporting adrenal gland function. The practice of scheduled food breaks during fasting helps control cortisol production, which prevents the body from experiencing excessive hormone peaks during the day. This balance fosters resilience against stress. Your body becomes better equipped to handle stress when it devotes fewer resources to digestion, thus reducing strain on your adrenal glands. The scheduled fasting times enable your body to restore itself while recovering from stress, which helps reduce the buildup of chronic stress. Your adrenal health benefits from fasting, leading to a peaceful lifestyle that effectively controls daily stress.

Calm, Rest, Adapt: Keys to Adrenal Balance

Maintaining adrenal health during fasting requires incorporating stress-reduction techniques into your daily routine. Integrate relaxation exercises throughout your daily activities. Deep breathing, combined with yoga and progressive muscle relaxation techniques, provides practical stress reduction benefits that support adrenal health. The activities decrease cortisol production, creating a state of relaxation. The same importance exists between getting enough rest and recovery. You must obtain sufficient sleep each night, as quality rest is a fundamental requirement for adrenal healing. Establish a bedtime routine by setting regular sleep and wake times, and prepare your bedroom for relaxation by reducing screen exposure before bedtime. Regular practice helps your body establish a balanced cortisol cycle, which supports your fasting and overall health.

Holistic health is the cornerstone of optimal adrenal support. By harmonizing fasting with lifestyle modifications, you establish a thorough approach to wellness. A nutritious diet rich in adaptogens and natural ingredients can enhance your body's ability to cope with stress. Adaptogens are natural substances, typically herbs, roots, and plant extracts, that help your body adapt to physical, emotional, or environmental stress. They support the body's homeostasis (balance) by regulating the hypothalamic-pituitary-adrenal (HPA) axis and other systems involved in stress response. Think of adaptogens as a thermostat for your body. When you're too "hot" (overstimulated or anxious), they help calm you down. When you're too "cold" (exhausted or sluggish), they help give you a natural energy boost.

Common Adaptogens and Their Key Benefits

- **Ashwagandha** - Reduces stress, calms anxiety, and supports thyroid and cortisol balance.
- **Rhodiola** - Boosts energy, focus, and endurance while supporting mental well-being and mood.

- **Holy Basil (Tulsi)** - Eases anxiety, supports immunity, and balances blood sugar.
- **Maca** - Balances hormones, improve libido, and supports mood.
- **Eleuthero (Siberian Ginseng)** - Boosts stamina, resilience, and focus.
- **Schisandra** - Supports liver health, endurance, and stress resilience.
- **Reishi Mushroom** - Calms the mind, supports immunity, and promotes longevity.
- **Cordyceps** - Enhance energy, stamina, and lung function.

Adaptogens are often taken as capsules or tablets, powders (for smoothies, teas, or lattes), tinctures, or tea. The addition of these ingredients to your food enhances the performance of your adrenal glands. The combination of lifestyle modifications and intermittent fasting creates an optimal environment for promoting adrenal health, leading to increased vitality and overall well-being.

BALANCING ESTROGEN: FASTING'S ROLE IN FEMALE HEALTH

Estrogen is like the quiet conductor of a complex orchestra, guiding countless processes that shape a woman's health, especially during the transformative years of menopause. While often overlooked, this powerful hormone plays a crucial role in maintaining balance across various bodily systems.

Estrogen preserves bone strength by regulating the natural process of bone remodeling, ensuring old bone is broken down, and new bone is rebuilt at a healthy rate. When estrogen levels decline, as they do during menopause, this protective effect weakens, leading to an accelerated loss of bone density. This is why women become more susceptible to osteoporosis and fractures, highlighting the importance of maintaining optimal estrogen levels for lifelong skeletal health.

Estrogen is also a defender of the heart and blood vessels. It helps regulate cholesterol by keeping LDL ("bad") cholesterol levels in check while boosting HDL ("good") cholesterol, which supports a healthy cardiovascular system. As estrogen levels drop during menopause, women's risk for heart disease increases, a leading cause of mortality among women.

Beyond the physical, estrogen has a powerful influence on the brain. It modulates the activity of key neurotransmitters, including serotonin, dopamine, and acetylcholine, which are critical for mood regulation, memory, focus, and cognitive performance. When estrogen levels fluctuate, many women experience brain fog, forgetfulness, difficulty concentrating, anxiety, and even depressive symptoms. This hormonal shift can impact both emotional resilience and mental sharpness, making it feel like your mind and mood are on a rollercoaster.

In short, estrogen is far more than a "reproductive hormone"—it's an essential regulator of whole-body health. Supporting healthy estrogen balance, whether through lifestyle, nutrition, or medical options, is crucial for preserving bone strength, protecting heart health, stabilizing mood, and maintaining cognitive clarity as women navigate the years beyond menopause.

Intermittent fasting offers a natural approach to help sustain healthy estrogen levels. A key benefit is its capacity to modulate estrogen receptors by improving the body's sensitivity to estrogen. As we have learned, fasting helps achieve hormonal balance. Moreover, fasting enhances detoxification pathways essential for processing and eliminating excess hormones. This mechanism ensures estrogen levels stay within a healthy range, preventing imbalances that can trigger various symptoms. Taking breaks from continuous digestion allows the liver, crucial for hormone metabolism, to operate more effectively. This improved efficiency can help regulate estrogen levels and foster a more balanced hormonal environment, which is particularly advantageous during and after menopause menopause.

A balanced diet supports fasting and helps maintain healthy estrogen levels. Incorporating cruciferous vegetables, such as broccoli, kale, and Brussels sprouts, into your meals can facilitate hormone metabolism. Vegetables contain compounds that help the body process and eliminate excess estrogen. Omega-3 fatty acids are also crucial in foods such as salmon, flaxseeds, and walnuts. Omega-3 fatty acids possess anti-inflammatory properties that support cardiovascular health and may improve mood. Adding these foods to your diet equips your body with the necessary nutrients for hormonal balance. This dietary strategy, when combined with intermittent fasting, creates an environment that is conducive to estrogen regulation.

Syncing Fasting with Your Cycle: Supporting Hormones Through Each Phase

Aligning your intermittent fasting schedule with your menstrual cycle can help support estrogen balance and reduce stress on the body. During the **follicular phase** (the first half of your cycle, starting with your period), estrogen levels rise, making it an ideal time for longer fasts, such as the 16:8 method, as energy and insulin sensitivity are typically higher. In contrast, during the **luteal phase** (the second half of the menstrual cycle, following ovulation), progesterone levels increase, and the body may require more calories and rest. This is a good time to shorten your fasting window to 12:12 or 14:10, or take a break altogether. Listening to your body and adjusting your fasting rhythm according to your cycle can enhance results, reduce cravings, and support a healthier, more sustainable fasting practice.

As we conclude our exploration of hormonal health in this chapter, it becomes clear that intermittent fasting offers numerous benefits for women over 50. From supporting estrogen balance to enhancing thyroid and adrenal health, fasting can play a pivotal role in navigating the changes that come with menopause. By embracing fasting alongside mindful dietary choices and lifestyle practices, you can promote a balanced hormonal environment that supports overall well-being. As we move forward, we'll delve into how fasting can aid in weight management and metabolic health, offering further strategies to enhance your vitality and quality of life.

3

WEIGHT MANAGEMENT AND METABOLIC HEALTH

T hink of wearing your favorite pair of jeans. The ones that make you look and feel like you can conquer the world. But lately, they've been feeling a bit snug, and you wonder whether it's just the dryer playing a trick on you or whether you're gaining weight. Many women in their 50s experience a slowdown in their metabolism, which can lead to weight gain. Our bodies change over time. While some changes are pleasant, others are not. The most significant change that can be observed is a decrease in our metabolic rate. The body, once a raging fire, is burning at a much slower pace.

METABOLIC SLOWDOWN: REVIVING YOUR METABOLISM WITH FASTING

This decline is not just a figment of our imagination but a real phenomenon that has been scientifically documented. Our basal metabolic rate (BMR) is the number of calories our body needs to perform its most basic life-sustaining functions while at complete rest. Our BMR reduces drastically as we age and enter the menopausal stage. As our estrogen levels decrease, so does our muscle mass. Muscles are said to be metabolically active, which implies that they can burn calories even if one is just watching television. As we age, we lose muscle mass, and our metabolic rate slows, which can lead to weight gain. In fact, after the age of 30, adults can lose 3–8% of their muscle mass per decade. While this natural progression is upsetting, recognizing it is the first step towards regaining control.

Firing Up Your Metabolism: How Fasting Triggers Thermogenesis

Intermittent fasting is one of the most refreshing ways to rejuvenate a slow metabolism. During your fasting periods, you help your body employ thermogenesis. The process by which your body produces heat. It's an essential part of your metabolism. This heat production helps regulate body temperature and burns calories in the process. It plays a significant role in controlling weight and maintaining energy balance. Increasing thermogenesis through Intermittent Fasting can help boost metabolism and support fat loss.

Boosting Metabolism: How Fasting Elevates Norepinephrine for Fat Burning

Intermittent fasting also helps to increase the levels of norepinephrine. Norepinephrine plays a decisive role in metabolism, especially as part of the sympathetic nervous system's "fight or flight" response. It helps mobilize energy quickly and boosts metabolic activity when your body needs it most. Norepinephrine increases calorie burn by stimulating thermogenesis, elevating the basal metabolic rate (BMR), and helping to burn more calories at rest. This combination can help prevent metabolic slowing down, making it easier to either maintain or lose weight. Fasting leverages the body's fat stores, making it easier for the body to burn fat as the practice progresses.

Another way to enhance and rejuvenate your metabolism is through high-intensity interval training (HIIT). This type of exercise is characterized by short and frequent activities with intervals of rest in between, and it is best done during your eating windows. HIIT burns calories during the workout and increases your metabolic rate for hours afterward.

REFLECTION EXERCISE: EVALUATE YOUR METABOLIC HEALTH

Take a moment to reflect on your lifestyle habits. Start a weekly log to track your meals, workouts, and hydration. It can be a great way to stay motivated. Pay attention to how your body responds after engaging in various activities and consuming different meals. This fun exercise can help you discover ways to boost your metabolism naturally. Understanding how your body reacts can help you tailor your fasting and exercise routines for optimal metabolic health.

By embracing these strategies, you can make a significant difference in overcoming metabolic slowdown, ultimately leading to a healthier and more energized version of yourself.

BREAKING THROUGH WEIGHT LOSS PLATEAUS

Have you ever had that feeling where you're putting in all the effort, but the scale just won't cooperate? You're in good company! Many women over 50 encounter those frustrating weight loss plateaus, where it seems like progress stalls despite their efforts. It's as if the body has adapted to its new routine, becoming more efficient and thus requiring fewer calories to maintain the same weight. This adaptation, combined with the hormonal changes that come with aging, can make it feel like you're stuck in a frustrating loop. The body, clever as it is, learns to conserve energy when it senses a prolonged decrease in calorie intake, making further weight loss challenging.

Breaking Plateaus: Using Fasting Flexibility to Reignite Your Metabolism

Intermittent fasting can be a fantastic friend in breaking through those plateaus. It keeps things exciting by shaking things up and ensuring the body doesn't become too comfortable with a routine. One practical approach is to vary your fasting windows. Adjusting your fasting and eating times can significantly help boost your metabolism and get your weight loss journey back on track. For example, if you usually stick to a 16:8 schedule, why not give extending your fasting period to 18 hours a shot? You can also have fun experimenting with a 5:2 approach, where you significantly reduce your calorie intake for two non-consecutive days each week. This variation keeps your body on its toes, helping it to access fat reserves and push past that plateau.

Calorie Cycling: Keeping Your Metabolism Flexible and Fasting Sustainable

You can also try cycling your calorie intake during your eating windows. Calorie cycling refers to the practice of varying your fasting schedule over time, either daily, weekly, or monthly, to better support your body's changing needs, especially in response to weight loss, hormone health, and long-term sustainability. This approach includes switching between days with higher and lower calorie intake. Some days, treat yourself to delicious, nutrient-packed meals with a few extra calories; on other days, go for lighter, well-balanced options that keep you feeling great. Cycling helps keep your body from getting stuck in a metabolic rut and encourages ongoing weight loss. Just as you need to vary your workout to keep seeing results, the same is true with intermittent fasting. Cycling also reduces cravings and binge urges. Taking a day or two each month to give yourself a little break from your fasting routine allows your body to rejuvenate, making it even more ready to jump back into fasting when you start again.

MARY'S INTERMITTENT FASTING RESET

Meet Mary, a 52-year-old teacher who has been practicing intermittent fasting (IF) for about 5 months. She followed a simple 16:8 routine. Fasting for 16 hours and eating during an 8-hour window, typically from 12:00 PM to 8:00 PM. Initially, the results were outstanding. Mary dropped 20 pounds, had more energy at school, and even noticed an improvement in her joint pain. However, after reaching the 3-month mark, progress stalled. No matter how disciplined she was, the scale remained stubbornly unchanged. Her clothes fit the same. Her energy dipped. Frustration crept in. One night, while scrolling through a health forum, she came across a post that resonated with her. "If you've plateaued, your body may have adapted. Shake things up, your schedule, your eating window, or your fasting length." That struck a chord. Mary realized she had been doing the same routine every single day. The same window, same meals, same calorie level. Perhaps her body had become too accustomed to it. So Mary made three simple changes:

1. **Switched to a 20:4 fast** three days per week (fasting for 20 hours, eating in a 4-hour window). On these days, she ate dinner between 4:00 and 8:00 PM, focusing on protein- and fiber-rich meals.
2. **Added one 24-hour fast per week** (from dinner one night to dinner the next). She did this on Mondays to mentally reset after the weekend.
3. **Started walking after his last meal**, even just 20 minutes. This light movement helped with insulin sensitivity and digestion.

Within two weeks, she started to see results. The scale began to move again, slowly but surely. Mary broke through the plateau and dropped another 6 pounds over the next month. More importantly, her energy returned, her sleep improved, and she felt in control again. She realized fasting wasn't just about the hours. It was about flexibility, adaptation, and listening to your body.

HOW JANE BROKE THROUGH HER FASTING PLATEAU

Jane was genuinely committed to her intermittent fasting routine, following a consistent 16:8 schedule for months. While she initially saw great results, she eventually hit a frustrating plateau. Her weight wouldn't budge, and her energy dipped. Rather than giving up, Jane decided to shake things up. She experimented with alternate-day fasting (ADF), where she fasted for 36 hours every other day, followed by a full day of mindful eating. She also began practicing calorie cycling, intentionally varying her intake between high and low-calorie days to keep her metabolism responsive.

Jane also added more protein to her meals and began eating earlier in the day on her eating days. Switching from a noon-to-8 p.m. window to a morning-to-afternoon window to support better insulin sensitivity. She also increased her daily movement, incorporating strength training twice a week to preserve muscle while burning fat. Within weeks, she noticed the scale moving again, her clothes fitting better, and her energy levels soaring.

These stories illustrate the importance of being flexible and trying new approaches in your fasting routine. Everyone's body is unique, so discovering what suits you best is super important. It's all about being open to exploring new methods, whether that's adjusting your fasting windows, experimenting with calorie cycling, or taking well-timed breaks. Just a quick reminder that a plateau isn't a setback; it's a chance to take a step back, make some tweaks, and keep pushing ahead. Embarking on the journey to health and wellness can be a challenging yet rewarding adventure, with its fair share of highs and lows.

However, remember that with the right tools and a positive mindset, progress is always just around the corner.

THE ART OF ENERGY SWITCHING FOR LIFELONG HEALTH

As we have learned, intermittent fasting is a key strategy for boosting metabolic flexibility. When your body switches between energy sources smoothly, you maintain stable blood sugar levels, avoid energy crashes, and stay on top of your weight management. Metabolic flexibility is like a well-oiled machine that runs smoothly regardless of the fuel you provide. When you fast, your body begins to use its fat stores for energy, a process known as fat oxidation. Fat oxidation is how your body "burns fat." It works by releasing fatty acids from fat cells into the bloodstream. These fatty acids are transported to tissues, such as muscle, where they are taken up by cells. Inside the cell's mitochondria (the "powerhouse"), fatty acids are then **oxidized** and combined with oxygen to create **ATP**, the energy your body uses to function.

Metabolic Flexibility helps you shed those extra pounds and boosts insulin sensitivity, which is crucial for maintaining stable blood sugar levels. Switching between fed and fasted states helps your body adapt to different energy sources, thereby boosting your metabolic efficiency. This flexibility helps keep your blood sugar levels in check, lowers the chances of insulin resistance, and provides steady energy throughout the day. It's like giving your metabolism a little boost, making it more responsive and efficient.

Want to boost your metabolic flexibility? Try integrating fasting with a low-carb diet. This combination encourages your body to prioritize fat as its primary fuel source. By reducing your carbohydrate intake during meals, you encourage your body to utilize its fat stores more efficiently. Regular exercise also plays a crucial role in improving metabolic shifts. Engaging in brisk walking, cycling, or swimming can train your metabolism to switch between fuel sources more efficiently. When these lifestyle changes are combined with fasting, they create a synergistic effect that can significantly enhance your body's adaptability and overall metabolic health. This strategy is a comprehensive approach that addresses weight management and promotes long-term health and vitality.

Studies have shown that being metabolically flexible is associated with a longer lifespan. Research shows that people with better metabolic adaptability tend to enjoy a longer health span, meaning they spend more years feeling good. Being adaptable can lower your chances of developing chronic issues like type 2 diabetes, heart disease, and obesity. Metabolic health pros say intermittent fasting is a great way to enhance flexibility. Fasting boosts your metabolism, making it easier to manage weight and live a healthier, longer life. It's like investing in a health plan that pays off in energy and overall well-being.

Metabolic flexibility sounds complicated, but really, it's just about helping your body adapt naturally. Boost your metabolism by incorporating fasting, a balanced diet, and regular exercise. Give it the tools to perform at its peak. It's not just about what or when you eat; it's about establishing a solid system that supports your health goals. If you want to lose weight, maintain your weight loss, or simply feel healthier, improving your metabolic flexibility can make a significant difference. It's all about finding that sweet spot, rolling with the punches, and setting the stage for a healthier future.

4

COGNITIVE AND EMOTIONAL
WELLNESS

few years ago, I attended a parent-visit day at my daughter's
high school. I recall being impressed by the amount of information the teachers provided to the kids and the expecta-
tions they had for them to learn in these 40-minute classes. That is
when I realized that my cognition had slowed a bit over the years. As we
age, maintaining mental sharpness can be a challenge. Recalling names
or even locating the remote control can be a struggle. Intermittent
fasting can help us regain clarity and boost our cognitive and emotional
well-being in some remarkable ways.

BRAIN BOOST: FASTING SPARKS NEUROGENESIS FOR
COGNITIVE CLARITY

Intermittent fasting extends beyond defining when to eat; it also significantly contributes to your brain's rejuvenation by boosting neurogenesis. Neurogenesis is the process by which new neurons (nerve cells) are
formed in the brain, thereby enhancing synaptic plasticity and
improving neuron communication. It's like a complete brain tune-up,
making those neural pathways work better than ever. These upgrades

can significantly improve your cognitive abilities, making it easier to locate your keys or follow the intricate plots in your favorite books. Aging slows down the brain's ability to create new cells and maintain strong connections, making intermittent fasting even more crucial.

Intermittent fasting can also significantly help reduce neuroinflammation, a key contributor to cognitive decline. This inflammation is the brain's immune response to various insults, which can lead to an escalation in the production of pro-inflammatory cytokines. Elevated levels of these molecules can deteriorate brain function and are associated with conditions such as Alzheimer's disease. Adding intermittent fasting to your daily routine can help lower inflammatory markers and create a more favorable environment for your brain to thrive.

BDNF Boost: How Fasting Fuels Memory, Learning, and Long-Term Brain Health

Fasting also enhances the production of brain-derived neurotrophic factor (BDNF), a crucial factor in memory and learning that helps maintain the health and growth of neurons. BDNF is like a magic potion for your brain, keeping it sharp and full of life. New research supports the theory that the brain-boosting benefits of intermittent fasting may enhance mental performance and reduce the risk of neurodegenerative diseases. Studies in animals have shown that fasting can improve memory and learning, likely due to increased levels of brain-derived neurotrophic factor (BDNF). Research on humans is still in its early stages, but the initial results appear promising. It seems that modulating BDNF through fasting may help slow cognitive decline. This suggests that fasting is not only beneficial for your body but also enhances your brainpower.

To minimize cognitive decline, consider timing your fasting periods with activities that require mental effort, as this can help maximize the benefit. If you have mornings filled with complex, brain-draining tasks, delaying breakfast to extend your fast may help you maintain mental clarity and focus. Adding brain-boosting foods to your meals during times of fasting can also significantly enhance these cognitive impacts. Omega-3s from salmon, walnuts, and flaxseeds are great for your brain, and antioxidants in leafy greens and berries help fight off cellular damage. Pairing these nutrients with intermittent fasting supercharges your brain, providing it with the fuel it needs to function optimally.

JOURNALING FOR CLEARER THINKING

Spend a few minutes at the end of every day, reflecting on your mental state before and after fasting. Do you ever notice those moments when your mind seems incredibly clear or concentrated? It is helpful to record any trends or shifts in a journal. This exercise helps you understand how fasting impacts your brain health, enabling you to adjust your regimen as needed. By taking control of your psychological well-being, you empower yourself and make decisions that truly improve your life.

Dive into these strategies and enjoy the ride to clearer thinking with an open heart and mind. It's all about finding what clicks for you and having fun taking care of your brain health.

ENHANCING MEMORY AND FOCUS WITH INTERMITTENT FASTING

Picture this: you're at your kitchen table, coffee in hand, and suddenly, your mind is sharp and clear, as if you've acquired a superpower. This isn't just a pipe dream; it's a real perk of intermittent fasting. Fasting enhances memory by stimulating brain pathways associated with learning. These pathways enhance your brainpower, helping you remember and retrieve information when you need it. The hippocampus is a small, seahorse-shaped structure located deep in the temporal lobe of the brain. It plays a critical role in memory, learning, and emotional regulation. This part of the brain is crucial for creating new memories and linking them to emotions, making it super essential for everyday life. Intermittent fasting enhances the function of your hippocampus, making it easier to learn and remember things. Pretty cool, right?

Sharper Mind, Longer Focus: How Fasting Supercharges Mental Clarity

Fasting also boosts your mental focus. When the body isn't constantly digesting, it frees up energy for the brain, increasing mental sharpness and focus. This usually means a longer attention span, helping you dive deeper into tasks without the usual distractions. Imagine getting lost in a book or a project, totally focused for hours on end. It also reduces mental fatigue, which can cloud your thinking and hinder productivity while boosting your mental resilience and leaving you feeling refreshed and empowered. This boost in mental stamina helps you tackle challenging tasks with ease, whether it's a tricky work project or just remembering where you parked your car.

Consider incorporating practical strategies into your fasting routine to maximize its benefits. Adding brain exercises, such as puzzles and brain games, can help keep your mind refreshed and sharp. These exercises activate your brain, forming new connections while also strengthening existing ones. Furthermore, dedicating fasting periods to tasks that need focus can efficiently enhance your productivity. When you have a project that requires concentration or a significant report to write, attempt to do it during your fasting periods when you're mentally most productive. That way, you can work more intelligently and precisely, making the most out of your heightened focus and mental acuity.

Feeding Your Focus: Pairing Fasting with Brain-Boosting Foods and Mental Exercises

Neuroscientists say that keeping your brain sharp with fasting isn't just about timing; it's also about what you put on your plate. A brain-boosting diet rich in antioxidants and healthy fats can help keep your mind sharp and ward off cognitive decline. Blueberries, kale, and avocados are rich in nutrients that support brain health and overall well-being. Additionally, nuts and seeds provide the healthy fats that keep your mind sharp. Adding these foods to your meals can enhance the benefits of fasting, helping your brain stay sharp and resilient.

Mental exercises and challenges are also of valuable importance. Engaging in activities that challenge your mind, such as a crossword puzzle or learning a new language, keeps your mind sharp and prepared for whatever challenges life throws your way. These exercises keep your brain fast and on its toes, ready to react, a key to mental sharpness later in life.

When you explore how fasting enhances brainpower, remember that every step you take to support your mind makes life more vibrant and focused. Syncing your fasting habits with your brain goals can boost your mental clarity and memory, making your daily life way better.

SLEEP AND FASTING: IMPROVING REST AND RECOVERY

When you hit the pillow, it's obvious just how crucial sleep is for your health. It's not just about closing your eyes at night; it's about letting your body recharge, heal, and get ready for tomorrow. A good night's sleep is key to feeling great, both physically and mentally. While you sleep, your brain is busy sorting through the day's events, locking in memories, and making room for new information. A solid night's sleep recharges you and gets you ready to tackle whatever comes your way. However, when your sleep is disrupted, it can significantly impact your brain, making it difficult to concentrate and remember things. Additionally, sleep and emotional health are closely linked. If you're not getting enough rest, you may end up feeling more on edge or anxious as your body tries to cope with stress.

Sleep Synergy: How Intermittent Fasting Aligns Your Body Clock for Better Rest

Intermittent fasting can actually boost your sleep quality by helping your body's internal clock align with the natural day-night cycle. This sync enables you to get better sleep by signaling to your body when it's time to wind down. When you start incorporating fasting into your routine, you may find that your sleep improves, with fewer nighttime wake-ups. When you eat, your last meal matters for making this better. Stop eating a few hours before bed, which gives your digestive system a chance to rest and makes it easier to fall asleep. This practice helps you fall asleep faster and stay in a deeper sleep throughout the night, thereby boosting your sleep quality and morning energy.

Research indicates that intermittent fasting can help alleviate sleep issues by supporting the body's natural circadian rhythms, reducing nighttime digestive activity, and stabilizing blood sugar levels, which in turn leads to deeper, more restorative sleep and a more refreshed, energized feeling in the morning.

Want to boost your sleep with fasting? Here are some easy tips to get you started. Start by syncing your eating times with your natural sleep cycle. If you're a night owl, a later eating schedule might be your jam, while early birds probably like to wrap up their meals before the sun goes down. Skip the big meals before bed; a full stomach can disrupt your sleep. Go for lighter, balanced meals that keep you feeling good and energized. Establishing a bedtime routine can significantly improve your sleep quality. Reading a book, soaking in a warm bath, or practicing relaxation techniques can signal to your body that it's time to unwind.

Take Sarah, for example. For years, she struggled with restless nights, tossing and turning, staring at the ceiling, and waking up groggy no matter how early she went to bed. Her mind would race, and her body never seemed to relax fully. After learning about the impact of late-night eating on sleep, Sarah decided to make a simple change. She moved her last meal to 6:00 p.m. and gave herself at least three hours before bed without food. The difference was remarkable. Within a week, she began falling asleep more easily, staying asleep longer, and waking up naturally without needing an alarm clock or caffeine. Her mornings felt lighter, her mood lifted, and for the first time in years, she felt truly rested and recharged.

James had a similar breakthrough. He used to rely on sleep aids and still found himself wide awake at 2 a.m. most nights. His eating schedule was inconsistent, with late dinners, nighttime snacking, and irregular routines that left his body confused and unbalanced. Once he adopted a consistent intermittent fasting schedule and stopped eating by 7:00 p.m., everything began to shift. His sleep patterns evened out. He woke up less during the midnight hours, had longer sleep cycles, and felt a wonderful sense of calm during the nighttime. James was sharp, awake, and emotionally level in the mornings, prepared to meet his day without that drowsy start that had been his norm.

These personal experiences illustrate the dramatic difference that seemingly small changes to your diet can make in both the quality of your sleep and how you wake up.

Reflect on the intricate interconnectedness of fasting, sleep, and health. One positive adjustment in a part of your life can have a significant impact on others, leading to a more balanced and satisfying experience. By aligning your fasting and sleeping habits, you improve your physical and mental well-being, setting yourself up for the vibrant life you deserve. With that, let us continue to examine how fasting aids in maintaining bone health and balancing our nutritional intake, which is essential for staying robust and healthy as we age.

EMOTIONAL EATING: STRATEGIES FOR CONTROL AND BALANCE

Emotional eating is a struggle that resonates with many of us. It's when we grab food not out of hunger but because we're stressed, anxious, bored, or feeling lonely. We've all grabbed a tub of ice cream after a tough day or mindlessly sat munching in front of the TV when we're feeling down. Emotional eating occurs when feelings take over instead of genuine hunger, and those emotions can be particularly potent triggers. Stress and anxiety usually lead us to seek out comfort foods for a quick fix of relief. Boredom often sends us to the pantry, hunting for something to munch on. At the same time, loneliness can lead us to reach for a bag of chips as a form of comfort.

Intermittent fasting provides a structured approach to breaking the habit of emotional eating. By establishing eating times through fasting, you create a system that makes senseless snacking less likely. This practice serves as a subtle reminder to pause and reflect. Are we hungry, or are we eating simply out of emotion or habit? Fasting helps us tune into our bodies and be more mindful about what we eat. Knowing your next meal is planned makes it way easier to focus on what you're eating instead of just grabbing whatever is available. Mindfulness can help us ditch emotional eating, allowing us to enjoy our meals with purpose and fully savor every bite.

Strategies to Tackle Emotional Eating Triggers

1. **Identify Your Triggers** - Understanding what triggers your emotions is crucial. Keep a journal to track your mood and eating habits, which can help you identify your feelings and understand what may trigger your snacking. Note your

emotions (such as boredom, stress, or loneliness), times of day, or specific situations.

2. **Pause and Breathe** - When you feel the urge to eat, pause for 5 minutes and take deep breaths. Ask yourself, *"Am I physically hungry or emotionally triggered?"*

3. **Practice Mindful Eating** - Eat slowly and without distractions (no TV or phone). Take time to savor each bite and focus on taste, texture, and how full you feel.

4. **Redirect the Energy** - Go for a walk, stretch, write, drink water, call a friend, read, or get into a hobby. Pick a self-calming activity that does not include food.

5. **Seek Help** - Consider consulting a therapist, coach, or joining a support group. You are not alone, and support can make all the difference.

JANICE'S STORY: FROM STRESS-EATING TO SELF-MASTERY

Take Janice, for example. A dedicated professional and busy mom, she found herself reaching for snacks every time work pressure spiked, or emotions ran high. It became a reflex, cookies when overwhelmed, and chips during tight deadlines. When she discovered intermittent fasting, everything changed. She began with a 14:10 schedule, gradually moving to a more consistent 16:8 routine.

Setting defined eating windows gave her structure and a sense of control that had been missing. With fewer opportunities to emotionally graze, Janice became more mindful about *why* she wanted to eat. She replaced stress-snacking with short walks, journaling, and deep breathing. Over time, she noticed not only a lighter body but a calmer mind. She felt emotionally stronger, more in tune with her needs, and no longer used food as a coping mechanism. For Janice, fasting became a form of self-care, not just a means of weight control.

LAURA'S STORY: SWAPPING SNACKS FOR SELF-DISCOVERY

Laura had a habit many of us can relate to: boredom eating. Evenings were her weak spot. After dinner, she'd drift to the kitchen without hunger, just looking for "something." That "something" usually turned into a handful of this and a scoop of that.

Fasting helped her break that cycle. By committing to a consistent eating window and respecting her body's natural hunger cues, she created space in her life for new habits. Instead of zoning out in front of the fridge, she started painting again—something she hadn't done since college. She tried yoga, joined a book club, and even began learning Spanish online. Laura discovered that what she was hungry for wasn't food; it was stimulation, connection, and a sense of purpose.

Fasting wasn't just a tool for physical health; it was a doorway to rediscovering joy.

MARIA'S JOURNEY: REBUILDING CONFIDENCE THROUGH CONSISTENCY

Then there's Maria, a 58-year-old grandmother who had spent years yo-yo dieting, always chasing the next "miracle" plan. She often felt defeated and disconnected from her body. When she started intermittent fasting, she didn't expect much—just a last-ditch attempt to feel more comfortable in her skin.

But the simplicity of it spoke to her. No counting, no guilt, just clear boundaries that helped her rebuild trust with food. She started with minor 12-hour fasts, then gradually extended them to 18:6. She paired her eating window with nourishing meals, walked every day, and reflected in a gratitude journal.

The result was noticeable not just on the scale. Maria felt strong and even gracious in her self-discipline. Her hunger pangs quieted, her skin radiated, and her inner critic softened. For the first time in years, she looked in the mirror and smiled—not because she was "perfect," but because she was at peace with the process.

These stories serve as reminders that intermittent fasting is not just a dietary shift—it's a profound shift in mindset. When combined with mindfulness and intention, it helps people reconnect with their bodies, break free from emotional eating, and rediscover parts of themselves they thought were lost.

These experiences demonstrate how intermittent fasting can enhance both physical health and emotional well-being. To build a better relationship with food, identify what triggers your emotional eating and tackle those head-on. Embracing mindfulness and establishing boundaries through fasting can significantly enhance your ability to live a more balanced and fulfilling life. It's all about enjoying food for its nourishment and pleasure, not using it as an emotional crutch.

5

BONE HEALTH AND
NUTRITIONAL BALANCE

P icture a house built on unstable ground, like peat or sand. Eventually, it will start to wobble and crack, struggling to handle the wear and tear from time and the elements. Bones are like the foundation of a house; they are essential for keeping our bodies stable and strong. As we age, maintaining strong bones is crucial, especially for women over 50. Our bones, once strong and sturdy, can start to weaken over time. In this chapter, we'll explore how to enhance your bone health through smart nutrition and simple strategies, allowing you to maintain a strong foundation for the future.

KEY NUTRIENTS FOR BONE HEALTH

When it comes to building and maintaining strong, healthy bones, especially as we age, three nutrients stand out above the rest: Calcium, Vitamin D, and Magnesium. These powerhouse nutrients work together to support bone density, structure, and function. Calcium acts as the primary building block of bone. Vitamin D helps the body absorb and use Calcium effectively, and Magnesium ensures that both are balanced and activated adequately within the body. Without the proper levels of all three, bones can become weak, brittle, and more prone to fractures over time.

Why Calcium is Crucial for Women Over 50

Calcium is essential for bone health. It builds and maintains bone density, much like steel beams in a skyscraper, providing structure and support. Calcium is the primary mineral stored in your bones and teeth, making your bones strong and sturdy. About 99% of the body's Calcium is found in the skeleton. Maintaining strong, healthy bones is the foundation for an active, independent life, especially as we age. Did you know that if we don't get enough Calcium, our bodies might start pulling it from our bones? This process can significantly increase the risk of osteoporosis and fractures. Your body is constantly breaking down old bone and building new bone. It's like a constant renovation project. Calcium is crucial for maintaining strong and sturdy bones during this process of renewal. Women over 50 should pay special attention to their bone health, as menopause can accelerate bone density loss due to the decline in estrogen levels. To get enough Calcium in your diet, you will need plenty of dairy products, such as milk, cheese, and yogurt. But if you're leaning towards a plant-based diet, tofu and fortified plant milks are fantastic alternatives. Women over 50 should aim to consume 1,200 mg of Calcium per day.

Vitamin D: The Key to Unlocking Calcium's Power

Vitamin D plays a crucial role in this process, helping your body absorb Calcium in the intestines. Think of it as the key that opens the door, letting Calcium in to strengthen your bones. Vitamin D enhances bone mineralization, ensuring that the Calcium you consume strengthens your bones. Vitamin D helps maintain muscle function and keeps your bones healthy, reducing the risk of falls and injuries. It is also crucial for helping your body absorb Calcium. It's like a gatekeeper, helping calcium move from the digestive tract into the bloodstream to strengthen bones.

A calcium-packed diet alone isn't enough for strong bones if you're not getting enough vitamin D. You can get this vitamin from foods like fortified cereals and fatty fish, including salmon and mackerel. Sunlight can also be a good source of Vitamin D, as exposure to the sun can naturally boost your body's vitamin D production. To maximize this benefit, plan to spend 10-30 minutes per day between 10 a.m. and 2 p.m., when UVB rays are strongest. While the sun is the best natural source of Vitamin D, excessive sun exposure increases the risk of skin cancer, so short exposure is key.

If you spend a lot of time indoors or live in an area with limited sunlight, consider taking Vitamin D supplements to help maintain healthy vitamin D levels. Women should aim for 800–1,000 IU of vitamin D per day.

Magnesium: The Unsung Hero of Bone Strength

Magnesium also plays a crucial role in bone health, working in tandem with Calcium to achieve optimal results. About 60% of the body's Magnesium is stored in the bones. It helps form the crystal structure of bones, keeping them dense and strong. It helps build bone mineralization, acting like a builder to keep everything solid and intact. Magnesium helps regulate calcium levels, preventing it from accumulating in soft tissues and ensuring it is directed into your bones.

How much Magnesium should you take each day? The recommended daily dose is 320 milligrams. However, many experts suggest 400–500 mg/day for therapeutic bone support, especially if you're also taking vitamin D and Calcium.

The best sources of Magnesium are spinach, Swiss chard, pumpkin seeds, almonds, avocados, black beans, and dark chocolate (yes, really!). Adding these to your meals can boost bone strength and improve your overall health. As we age, we're more likely to miss out on essential nutrients due to changes in our eating habits and the way our bodies absorb nutrients. It's necessary to pay attention to what we're eating. Not getting enough key nutrients can weaken our bones, increasing the risk of fractures and breaks. Incorporating a variety of nutrient-rich foods is a smart way to maintain healthy bones.

Simple Ways to Get Bone-Building Nutrients Every Day

Getting these nutrients into your daily routine can be easier than you think! Kick off your day with fortified orange juice, an easy way to boost your breakfast and get your vitamin D. Pair it with plant-based milk like Cashew, Almond, or Oat, and whole-grain cereals for a solid breakfast combo that provides the Calcium and Vitamin D you need for strong bones. For lunch or dinner, try whipping up some leafy green salads with almonds and a sprinkle of cheese to boost your calcium and magnesium intake. Or consider adding sardines to your meals for an added nutritional boost. These fish pack a punch with Vitamin D and omega-3 fatty acids, giving you some serious health perks. Yogurt and cheese are tasty ways to boost your calcium intake, making them excellent snacks or great additions to a balanced meal.

These foods are incredibly versatile, which is what makes them so awesome. Think of every meal as an opportunity to boost your bone health. Focusing on these nutrients helps increase your bone strength, allowing you to stay active and independent. The strength you build now will pay off later, giving you a solid foundation of endurance and energy. Incorporate these nutrients into your daily routine to boost your body's defenses and live a vibrant, healthy life.

REFLECTION EXERCISE: BUILDING A BONE-HEALTHY MEAL PLAN

Included in your bonus material is a weekly meal plan rich in bone-boosting nutrients. It includes foods that are rich in calcium, Vitamin D, and magnesium. I encourage you to make your own weekly meal plan. Vary your ingredients daily for a well-balanced plate. This exercise demonstrates how to easily incorporate essential nutrients into your diet, making bone health both tasty and achievable. As you explore these strategies, remember that taking care of your bones is a smart move for your overall health. It gives you the strength and stability to enjoy all life's adventures fully.

THE ROLE OF PROTEIN IN MAINTAINING BONE STRENGTH

Most people don't think of protein when it comes to strong bones, but it's super important for bone health. Protein makes up the framework that keeps them strong and structured. It's like the scaffolding of a building, giving it strength and stability. If you don't get enough protein, your bone structure can weaken, raising the chances of bone problems. Women over 50 need to ensure they're getting enough protein to maintain strong bones and well-shaped muscles. Strong muscles act as a safety net for your bones, providing them with support and cushioning to help prevent fractures and falls. As we age, we naturally lose muscle mass, so it's essential to incorporate protein-rich foods into our diet to combat this decline and maintain bone health.

Powering Your Fast: Protein Strategies for Strong Bones and Muscles

Finding protein sources that easily fit into your fasting schedule is crucial for maintaining healthy bones and muscles. Chicken and turkey are fantastic sources of high-quality protein. They pack a solid protein punch without all the extra fats, making them perfect for keeping your diet on point. These meats are incredibly versatile and can be cooked in various ways to keep your meals fun and delicious. If you're into plant-based eats, lentils and quinoa are fantastic choices. Lentils pack a punch with protein and fiber, helping to support digestion and keep you satisfied for longer. Quinoa is a superfood rich in complete protein, providing all nine essential amino acids your body needs. Plant-based proteins are a great way to get the nutrients you need while keeping your meals interesting and varied.

Getting enough protein during meals requires some planning, but it's doable! Be sure to include protein in every meal. This practice helps maintain your protein levels and supports the repair and growth of your muscles throughout the day. If you're struggling to get enough protein from your meals, consider adding protein supplements to your diet. Protein powders are a quick and easy way to boost your protein intake, especially when added to smoothies or yogurt. Protein shakes are a convenient and fast way to boost your protein intake on the go. My favorite protein shake is the Owyn brand. They come in many flavors and include 12-30 grams of protein, depending on the flavor you choose. Both protein powders and shakes offer a fast and straight-forward way to boost your protein intake, eliminating the hassle of cooking a full meal, making them perfect for busy days or when you're fasting.

Discover these high-protein meal ideas that perfectly complement your fasting plan. Grilled chicken with quinoa and veggies is a tasty and healthy meal. Chicken gives you lean protein, and quinoa throws in some plant-based protein and essential amino acids. Add some colorful veggies for a boost of vitamins and minerals, creating a dish that's great for your bones and muscles. Lentil soup with whole-grain bread? Yes, please! This soup packs a protein and fiber punch, and the bread provides complex carbs to keep your energy levels up. This combo is super hearty, filling, and a breeze to whip up—perfect for any meal.

Adding these protein-packed meals to your routine can boost your bone strength. Increasing your protein intake from a variety of sources helps keep your body strong and healthy. These food choices support your bone health and keep you feeling great, allowing you to live life to the fullest. As we seek ways to stay healthy, remember that even the most minor changes can add up to aging well.

FASTING-FRIENDLY FOODS FOR BONE DENSITY

The foods we choose play a crucial role in maintaining the strength and health of our bones. Choosing the right foods when you break your fast or eat during your window can significantly impact your bone health. Spinach and kale are not only delicious but also packed with nutrients that are beneficial for your bones. These greens pack a calcium punch for strong bones and are loaded with antioxidants. Antioxidants play a crucial role in combating oxidative stress, which can damage cells, including those essential for building and maintaining bone tissue. A diet rich in antioxidants can enhance your overall health and help strengthen and make your bones more resilient.

Nuts and seeds are a powerhouse for bone health, especially rich in Magnesium and phosphorus. These minerals are essential for building and maintaining strong bones as you age. Magnesium is packed in almonds and sunflower seeds, and it helps your body make the most of Calcium. Plus, phosphorus teams up with Calcium to strengthen your bones. Healthy fats help your body absorb all the vitamins and minerals, ensuring you get the most out of the nutrients in your food. Adding mixed nuts or seeds to your daily routine provides a tasty crunch and a solid nutritional boost.

PREPARING BONE-FRIENDLY MEALS

Now comes the fun part! Preparing meals with bone-friendly foods is both enjoyable and beneficial for your health. This kale and almond salad, which is drizzled with a zesty citrus vinaigrette, is a delicious way to get your calcium and magnesium fix. Almonds bring a crunchy vibe and some good fats, and that citrus dressing? It helps your body absorb all the nutrients more effectively. Also, try a spinach and feta stuffed chicken breast for a heartier meal. This dish packs protein, leafy greens, and calcium-rich cheese into one tasty meal that's great for your bones and your taste buds. These delicious meal ideas will fit perfectly into your fasting routine, providing you with the fuel you need without the heaviness.

Adding these foods to your routine, even while fasting, takes a bit of planning, but it is doable. Getting meals ready in advance means you'll have healthy options on hand, even when life gets hectic. Whipping up a big batch of salad or prepping stuffed chicken breasts in advance lets you zero in on your fasting goals while still eating right. Bone-friendly snacks, such as roasted nuts, are great for keeping you full and satisfied during your eating windows. These snacks are portable and perfect for a quick, healthy bite when hunger hits.

Putting in the effort to plan and whip up nutrient-rich meals for your bones isn't just about sticking to a diet; it's a promise to your long-term health. When you're weighing your choices, remember that variety is key. Adding a mix of greens, nuts, and seeds can significantly enhance your meals and boost their nutritional value. Your bones are the back-bone of your body, and by feeding them the right foods, you set yourself up for a healthier, more active life. This strategy amplifies the benefits of intermittent fasting, enabling you to take control of your health.

MAKE A DIFFERENCE WITH YOUR REVIEW

Unlock the Power of Generosity

"The best way to find yourself is to lose yourself in the service of others." –
Mahatma Gandhi

When we give without expecting anything back, life feels fuller and more joyful. That's what makes generosity so powerful.

Would you help another woman—someone just like you—who is curious about intermittent fasting but doesn't know where to begin?

My mission with this book is simple: to make intermittent fasting easy, clear, and doable for women over 50. But I can't reach everyone on my own. I need your help.

Here's the truth: most people decide whether to read a book based on reviews. That means *your words matter.* By leaving a short review, you can guide another woman to take that first step toward feeling stronger, more energetic, and more confident in her body.

Your review could help...

- One more woman discovers the freedom of fasting.
- One more grandmother feels energized to play with her grandkids.
- One more friend finally took control of her health.
- One more person believes it's never too late to thrive.

It doesn't cost anything, and it takes less than a minute—but it can change someone's journey.

☞ Simply scan the QR code below and leave your review:

[https://www.amazon.com/review/review-your-purchases/?asin= BOOKASIN]

If you believe in lifting others up, then you're exactly the kind of person who inspires me to keep writing. From the bottom of my heart, thank you for helping me spread this message of hope, health, and vitality.

With gratitude,

Claudia Von

6

DIGESTIVE HEALTH AND FASTING

Picture your digestive system as a lively city, with roads and pathways connecting every part of your body. Your gut health is like a city with clear streets; everything runs smoothly when it's balanced and working right. If you're over 50, maintaining a healthy gut is crucial for optimal digestion and overall well-being. Intermittent fasting is a game-changer for your digestive health, making it a must-have in your wellness arsenal.

IMPROVING GUT HEALTH WITH FASTING

Your gut microbiome is like a bustling city, packed with trillions of bacteria that keep your digestive system running smoothly. It affects everything from digestion to immunity and even your mood. Intermittent fasting promotes gut health by fostering a diverse and balanced microbiome. Fasting provides your body with an opportunity to reset and address gut inflammation, which can have a subtle yet significant impact on your overall health. Allowing your digestive system to rest helps good bacteria flourish. This thriving microbiome helps produce vital nutrients, such as B vitamins and vitamin K, which are essential for maintaining good health as we age.

Fasting enhances gut health by improving digestive efficiency. When your digestive system isn't constantly busy with food, it can absorb nutrients more effectively. This means that when you eat, your body can absorb and utilize the vitamins and minerals it needs more effectively. Additionally, fasting can improve bowel regularity, which is particularly important for many women over 50. Fasting helps keep your digestion on track, ensuring everything flows smoothly and reducing bloating or discomfort. Fasting can significantly boost your digestive health. It's a game-changer.

Studies have shown that fasting has a positive impact on the gut microbiome. Intermittent fasting enhances gut health by increasing beneficial bacteria, such as Akkermansia muciniphila, thereby making your microbiota more diverse and balanced. Akkermansia muciniphila is one of the beneficial bacteria that live in the mucus layer of your intestines. It plays a crucial role in maintaining gut health. It has become a focus of interest in microbiome and longevity research.

Research indicates that fasting can help alleviate gastrointestinal issues, underscoring its potential as a natural remedy for digestive health. More studies are needed to understand these benefits fully. Still, the current evidence suggests that fasting may significantly enhance gut health.

Want to boost your gut health? Start with a 16:8 fasting plan. This schedule works well with your body's natural rhythms and helps your digestion.

REFLECTION SECTION: LISTENING TO YOUR GUT

Consider how your digestion is functioning at the moment. Consider starting a journal to track changes in your digestion, bowel movements, and energy levels as you incorporate fasting into your routine. This practice helps you identify patterns and adjust your fasting regimen to enhance your gut health. Understanding your digestive system enables you to make informed choices for your health.

FOODS TO SUPPORT DIGESTIVE WELLNESS

Think of your gut as a little garden inside your body, full of tiny workers that keep you feeling your best. Like any good garden, it needs the right mix of seeds, fertilizer, and tools to thrive. Probiotics are the seeds to plant good bacteria. Prebiotics are the fertilizer, feeding those bacteria so they can grow strong. And fiber? That's your gardener's toolkit, keeping everything neat and balanced. With the right mix of these nutrients in your meals, you can create a healthy, happy gut that supports better digestion, boosts energy, and keeps you thriving from the inside out.

Probiotics: Planting the Seeds of a Healthy Gut

Probiotic-packed foods, such as yogurt and kefir, are like enthusiastic gardeners, bringing in beneficial bacteria to keep your gut in balance. Probiotics are live "good" bacteria that support a healthy gut. These tiny living organisms help to maintain balance in your digestive system by promoting the growth of beneficial bacteria and keeping harmful microbes in check. Adding yogurt or kefir to.your daily routine is a delicious way to maintain a balanced diet. It adds a creamy texture to your meals that are both super satisfying and beneficial for your gut.

Prebiotics: Fertilizer for a Thriving Gut

Probiotics aren't the only stars in this mix. Garlic and onions are excellent prebiotic foods that nourish the beneficial bacteria in your gut. They're like fertilizer for your gut, helping it thrive and flourish. These foods contain fibers that your body cannot break down, but your gut bacteria can. When they break down these fibers, they create compounds that are great for your colon cells and boost gut health. Adding garlic to your meals or incorporating onions into your salads is a simple way to enhance your gut health.

Fiber: The Gardener's Toolkit for Digestive Health

Fiber is essential for maintaining a healthy digestive system. It's like the gardener's toolkit, keeping everything neat. There are two types of dietary fiber: soluble and insoluble. Soluble fiber found in foods like oats and apples mixes with water to create a gel-like substance. This helps regulate your blood sugar levels and lower cholesterol. It helps keep your bowels regular by soaking up water and adding bulk to your stools, making them easier to pass. Insoluble fiber, which you get from whole grains and legumes, helps bulk up your stool and speeds up food moving through your stomach and intestines. This fiber is excellent for preventing constipation, especially as we age.

Incorporating gut-friendly foods into your daily meals can be fun and straightforward. Start your morning with overnight oats topped with chia seeds and berries. This dish contains a substantial amount of soluble fiber, enhancing both its flavor and nutritional value. Try a salad with kimchi and carrots for lunch or dinner. It's got a zesty kick and a probiotic boost. These meals are not only delicious but also packed with nutrients that are great for your gut health.

When planning your meals, try to balance your intake of probiotics and prebiotics. Prebiotics are like the fertilizer for your gut. They nourish the garden (microbiome), allowing it to grow strong and diverse. Probiotics are like the seeds in your gut. They introduce new plants (good bacteria) into the garden to help it flourish. This combo gives the good bacteria in your gut the fuel they need to thrive. Incorporating a variety of colorful veggies into your diet boosts fiber diversity. It helps maintain a balanced diet for improved digestive health. Leafy greens, bell peppers, and carrots not only make your meals visually appealing but also boost your fiber intake, which is beneficial for gut health.

MANAGING BLOATING AND IRREGULARITY

Imagine you just had a fantastic meal, but now you're feeling all bloated and uneasy. We all get it, right? Bloating and irregularity can strike us unexpectedly, leaving us feeling sluggish and out of sync. Women over 50 often experience digestive issues more frequently. There are several reasons why this happens. Overeating can significantly distend the stomach, leading to some discomfort. Mixing proteins and heavy starches? Well, that's a surefire way to invite digestive problems. Stress is a factor, too. When things get chaotic, digestion is often the first to suffer, slowing down and developing irregularities. Being well-hydrated is also necessary. If you do not take enough fluids, your digestive system slows down. Thus, your body is not able to eliminate waste effectively.

Intermittent fasting is a great way to address these issues. Fasting gives your digestive system a break, letting it repair and recharge. When you're fasting, your body does more than just digest food. It focuses on healing and maintenance, which significantly reduces bloating. Taking a break can help your gut reset, allowing it to work more efficiently when you eat. Fasting helps keep your bowels moving smoothly by boosting gut motility. Eating at set times helps your digestive system get into a groove, making your bowel movements more regular. This boost in motility helps food move through your digestive tract, reducing bloating and promoting regular bowel movements.

What is the best way to manage these symptoms? Start adding fiber-packed foods gradually during your meal times. Fiber is key to keeping your digestion running smoothly. But remember, don't go overboard too quickly—it might make you uncomfortable, so ease into it gradually. Start your day with soluble fiber sources, such as oats, to help soften your stools and make them easier to pass. Start incorporating whole grains into your diet to keep things running smoothly. Staying hydrated is super important. Staying hydrated throughout the day helps keep your digestive system running smoothly and reduces the risk of constipation. Peppermint and ginger herbal teas are great for digestion and can help you chill out.

Making adjustments to your lifestyle can significantly improve your digestive comfort. Mindful eating is a great strategy to try out. Eating mindfully and taking the time to chew can help you swallow less air, which in turn results in less bloating. Take your time with each bite and set your fork down between mouthfuls. This one adjustment to your mealtime can make a significant impact on the way you eat, help digestion along, and alleviate discomfort. Be active. Regular walking or light exercising can greatly assist digestion, help regulate bowel movements, and minimize bloating. By moving your body, you allow food to pass smoothly through the digestive tract, giving it a gentle nudge.

Look at incorporating light stretching or yoga into your daily routine. Not only will these improve your physical health, but they also help digestion by easing tension and stress. Because stress can significantly impact digestion, it is essential to find effective ways to control it. Chill out with meditation, soak up some nature, or dive into a hobby; cutting down on stress can seriously boost your happiness levels.

These handy tips, along with intermittent fasting, can make your digestion smoother and more regular. Listen to your body! Notice how it reacts to different foods and habits, and you'll be able to craft a personalized plan that boosts your digestion and overall health.

UNDERSTANDING THE GUT-BRAIN CONNECTION

Picture a hectic highway zipping between your gut and brain, always buzzing with messages. The gut-brain axis is like a communication superhighway, showing just how connected our bodies are. It's pretty fascinating and complex. The vagus nerve is the key player here, a long and twisty nerve that serves as the main highway for these messages. Think of it as a phone line where your gut and brain can talk about everything from digestion to your mood. A healthy gut sends positive signals to your brain, boosting your mood and mental well-being. When things are off balance, it can totally mess with your mood, leading to anxiety or even depression. It really demonstrates how significantly your gut health affects your mental state.

Intermittent fasting really boosts the gut-brain connection. Fasting boosts gut health, which means your brain gets better signals that support your mental well-being. A healthier gut can actually help reduce anxiety and depression because a balanced microbiome produces mood-boosting neurotransmitters. When your gut flora is happy, it boosts serotonin production, the "feel-good" hormone. You'll feel happier and sharper, staying alert, focused, and emotionally balanced. Fasting allows your gut to heal and find its balance, reducing inflammation and helping you think more clearly.

Research reveals the significant importance of this connection. Probiotics, the good bacteria in some foods, can seriously boost your mood and mental health, according to studies. These studies show that taking probiotics might boost your mood and help ease anxiety and depression symptoms. The gut-brain axis is connected through various pathways, including the immune system and neurotransmitter production, which influence our emotions. A healthy gut means these pathways function more effectively, resulting in a more stable mood and clearer thinking. Scientists are exploring this connection, excited about how gut health could revolutionize mental health treatment.

There are numerous ways to strengthen this vital connection in your life. Start your day off by incorporating fermented foods into your meals. Think sauerkraut, kimchi, and kombucha. These foods are rich in probiotics that help maintain a healthy gut microbiome, thereby enhancing your digestion and mental well-being. Fermented foods boost your gut flora, adding the variety it needs to thrive. Diet tweaks and stress-busting techniques can really boost your gut and brain health. Meditation, deep breathing, and yoga are excellent ways to relax and reduce stress, which is beneficial for your digestion. Managing stress helps keep your gut in check and boosts that gut-brain connection.

As you learn about the gut-brain connection, consider how these tips can be integrated into your everyday life. What you consume and how you deal with stress can significantly enhance your gut-brain connection and your overall well-being. This single-step solution boosts mental health and leads to a more energetic, balanced life. Summing up this chapter, we have explored the fascinating ways in which our gut and brain are connected, illustrating just how much impact our digestive health has on our mind. Having this connection established helps us make intelligent choices for our body and mind.

7

PRACTICAL IMPLEMENTATION
AND MEAL PLANNING

Your journey with intermittent fasting is all about finding renewed energy and wellness. Picking the right eating window is just like finding the best time for a stroll. Align your schedule with your natural rhythms to maximize the benefits of intermittent fasting.

CHOOSING THE RIGHT FASTING PROTOCOL

Creating a personalized fasting plan is like designing a custom dress that fits you perfectly. It amps up your comfort and confidence, keeping you committed and motivated. Tailoring your fasting plan allows you to incorporate what you enjoy while pursuing your health goals. Being adaptable is key to fitting intermittent fasting into your life.

Begin by taking a close look at your lifestyle, considering your daily routines, level of activity, and social commitments. This will help you create a fasting plan that fits you perfectly. This analysis enables you to identify when your energy peaks and the optimal times to fast, making it a seamless fit into your lifestyle.

When selecting the best fasting schedule, consider how it will fit into your lifestyle and align with your personal health goals. Ask yourself the following questions and complete the self-assessment questionnaire included at the back of this book to determine which fasting protocol works best for you.

1. What are the goals you are trying to achieve with Intermittent Fasting?
2. When do you have the most energy?
3. Is your schedule variable with numerous social commitments? Or do you prefer routine and structure?

Conside your health objectives. Are you trying to manage your weight, increase your energy levels, or improve your metabolic health? Your goals can help you decide which protocol will work best for your situation.

Next, choose an eating window that aligns with your energy highs and significantly boosts your fasting performance. For many people, mornings are when they feel most energized and ready to tackle the day's challenges. At the same time, others get a boost of energy in the afternoon or evening. Hence, a later eating window works better for them. Pay attention to your natural energy cycles to determine an eating window that supports your fasting goals and aligns with your daily activities. It's all about finding that perfect balance between your body's needs and your lifestyle.

Finally, consider your schedule. Do you have a variable schedule with numerous social commitments during the week? To make Intermittent Fasting work, it's essential to consider your schedule and social plans. If you have a packed schedule that starts early, starting your eating window in the morning could be the best approach. This timing allows you to tap into your morning energy boost, providing the fuel you need to stay sharp and lively for the day ahead. If your evenings are filled with family dinners or social hangouts, picking an eating window later in the day might work better for you. This tweak makes intermittent fasting fit seamlessly into your life, enhancing your routine instead of disrupting it. If flexibility and customization are essential in making fasting work for you, the 16:8 approach may be most effective. If, on the other hand, you prefer routine and structure, then the 5:2 or alternate-day fasting protocols may be more suitable for you.

Trying out different fasting schedules is key to making your intermittent fasting journey work for you. Starting with a 12-hour eating window is an easy way to begin your fasting journey. Kick off your day with a healthy breakfast at 8 a.m. and wrap up your eating with dinner by 8 p.m. This schedule aligns perfectly with our usual daily routine, making it extremely easy to get started.

As you become accustomed to this new routine and feel more confident in your fasting, you may want to narrow your eating window to enhance the benefits further. Switching to a 10-hour eating window means starting your day with breakfast at 9 a.m. and concluding it with dinner by 7 p.m. It's a more compact schedule but still allows you to enjoy balanced meals throughout the day. If you're up for a challenge, try an 8-hour window to ramp up your fasting game. Try eating between 10 a.m. and 6 p.m. to sync your meals with daylight. Many people say it boosts their energy and metabolism.

Experimenting is key to perfecting your fasting plan. Listen to your body when you fast. See how it reacts to different lengths and tweak it to what feels good for you. Seasonal shifts can affect your fasting game. You may find yourself wanting shorter fasting windows during the colder months when your body craves extra energy. Stay flexible and prepared for change; consider fasting as a vital part of your overall health regimen. Try out different approaches and pay attention to how your body feels. You'll have a fasting plan tailored to your health goals and designed to enhance your quality of life.

Consider combining intermittent fasting with specific diet styles to enhance its health benefits. Combining intermittent fasting with a low-carb diet can significantly improve weight loss and help regulate blood sugar levels. Combining fasting with the Mediterranean diet, renowned for its heart-healthy fats, an abundance of fruits and vegetables, and lean proteins, can significantly enhance your heart health and overall well-being.

REFLECTION SECTION: FINDING YOUR IDEAL EATING WINDOW

Reflect on your daily routine and how your energy levels fluctuate throughout the day. Pay attention to when you're most awake and when you start to feel sluggish. Experiment with different eating windows and record your experiences in a journal. This exercise helps you identify patterns and choose an eating window that enhances your energy and overall well-being. Listen to your body! It enables you to craft a fasting routine that perfectly suits your needs and lifestyle.

TOOLS AND TIPS TO STAY ON TRACK

Sticking to a regular intermittent fasting routine is key to reaping the most benefits from it. Start by carefully preplanning your meals and fasting intervals ahead of time, having a clear idea of what you'll eat and when you'll be able to avoid decision fatigue, which will allow you to be more consistent.

Using Tracking Tools and Apps to Stay on Track with Fasting

Tracking tools and apps can provide additional support by sending reminders and allowing you to track your progress. The best apps for intermittent fasting are Zero and Fastic, but Life Fasting Tracker and MyFitnessPal are also excellent choices. Zero is the best timer because it is simple and fast. It tracks your fasts, syncs with health apps, and visualizes your progress. This is the one if you want a clean and motivating visual tracker. Fastic is the best for habit-building. It includes hydration reminders, step counting, and education tips. If you need more encouragement, Fastic also provides "badges" and streak tracking to keep you motivated. For community support, try Life Fasting Tracker. It tracks fasting and provides the option to join groups for accountability. MyFitnessPal also tracks your fasting and food intake. Still, it has the added feature of effortlessly combining fasting with macronutrients and calorie tracking. For those who prefer the low-tech approach and use the pencil-and-paper method, a tracking journal is located at the back of this book. Using either an app or a tracking journal to track your progress will provide valuable insights into your fasting regimen. With data-driven results, you can make the most effective adjustments to achieve optimal outcomes. This systematic plan keeps you committed to your objectives while building a firm foundation for success.

CRAFTING BALANCED MEALS FOR YOUR EATING WINDOW

Finding the right balance is crucial when you're fueling up during your eating windows. Your meal is like a symphony, where every nutrient plays a role in maintaining a balanced body. Protein, fats, and carbs are your main macronutrients. They give you the energy and building blocks your body craves. Protein is essential for maintaining strong muscles and healthy cells, especially as you age. Chicken, fish, tofu, and legumes are excellent sources of lean protein. Fats get a bad rap, but they're essential for making hormones and keeping your brain in top shape. Avocados, nuts, seeds, and olive oil are packed with healthy fats that fuel your body. Carbs are your body's primary energy source, so grab them from whole grains, fruits, and veggies. These sources provide the energy you need and pack in the fiber necessary for digestion and a feeling of fullness.

Building Balanced Meals with the Plate Method

Creating balanced meals may seem challenging at first, but it becomes much easier with a solid plan. The **Plate Method** is a simple, visual approach to building balanced, nutritious meals, without the need to count calories or track macros. It's especially helpful for improving portion control, managing blood sugar, and supporting overall health. Picture a standard 9" plate divided into sections, with each part dedicated to a different food group, ensuring a balanced meal. Start by loading half your plate with a mix of vibrant vegetables. These vibrant colors aren't just visually appealing; each one contains a powerful blend of vitamins and minerals that your body needs. Leafy greens, bell peppers, and eggplants are great additions to your meals. They pack in nutrients, bring fun variety, and are low in calories, so you can enjoy bigger portions without feeling guilty.

Then fill up a quarter of your plate with lean proteins. This part is crucial for maintaining our muscle strength, especially as we age. You've got options like grilled chicken, baked salmon, tofu, and legumes. They're loaded with protein and keep you feeling full and satisfied for a long time. This really helps keep hunger in check while you're fasting.

Fill the last quarter of your plate with whole grains or starchy vegetables, such as quinoa, sweet potatoes, or brown rice. These foods serve as your energy boosters, providing a steady flow of energy and fiber, which is essential for a healthy gut and keeping you feeling full. Choosing whole, minimally processed foods significantly boosts your nutrient intake. Whole foods, whether natural or nearly so, offer a wealth of nutritional benefits. They're typically packed with more nutrients and fewer calories than processed foods, making them an excellent choice for maintaining a healthy diet and staying energized.

Mixing a variety of whole foods in your meals provides a wealth of nutrients. It adds interesting textures and flavors, making your food more enjoyable and delicious. Stick to this easy framework, and you'll whip up balanced, nutritious meals that boost your intermittent fasting game and help you feel great for the long haul.

Delicious Meal Combinations for Balanced Nutrition and Flavor

Let's explore some delicious meal combinations that strike the perfect balance of nutrition and flavor, sparking your culinary creativity. Imagine this: a plate piled high with fluffy quinoa next to perfectly grilled salmon, glistening with a touch of olive oil. Surrounding this centerpiece is a colorful mix of roasted vegetables – golden-brown Brussels sprouts, sweet red bell peppers, and tender asparagus, all tossed with a touch of garlic and extra-virgin olive oil. Quinoa packs a punch with complete protein and fiber, and that omega-3-loaded salmon? It's a win for your heart and brain. The veggies pack a punch of vitamins and minerals, offering a mix of textures and flavors that make every bite both tasty and enjoyable.

Try a chickpea salad for a tasty, plant-based option that's refreshingly delicious. Picture a bowl packed with fresh mixed greens, juicy cherry tomatoes, and crunchy cucumbers; all topped off with hearty chickpeas. A splash of top-notch olive oil and a squeeze of fresh lemon juice give the salad a tasty boost without taking over the flavors. This meal packs a serious nutritional punch with a great combo of fiber, plant protein, and healthy fats. Chickpeas are incredibly satisfying and packed with essential amino acids; olive oil adds those heart-healthy monounsaturated fats.

If you love a slight sweetness but want to stay healthy, grab some fresh fruit and a handful of nuts; it's the perfect snack combo. Imagine a bowl bursting with juicy berries, crunchy apple slices, sweet peach wedges, and a sprinkle of almonds, walnuts, or pistachios. This snack is a tasty treat that provides a quick energy boost from natural sugars, fiber for digestion, and a balanced mix of healthy fats and proteins from the nuts, keeping you full and supporting your muscles.

Explore these meal and snack ideas to kickstart your culinary adventures. They nail-balanced nutrition by combining protein, fats, and carbs to help you achieve your health goals while keeping your taste buds satisfied. You can whip up endless tasty and healthy meals, so dive into the incredible flavors and nutrients food has to offer.

Switching up your meals is key to keeping things interesting and making sure you get all the nutrients you need. Vary your winter, spring, summer, and autumn fruits and vegetables to keep your meals engaging and dynamic. There are treats in each season, such as luscious summer berries or warming winter squash. Global cuisine can add a new twist to your meal with exotic, bold flavors and textures. Add a sprinkle of turmeric or cumin for an Indian flair, or mix in miso or sesame oil for an Asian flair. Not only do these ingredients and spices enhance the taste, but they also offer significant health advantages. Add excitement to your meals and boost your nutrition by trying new foods.

EASY RECIPES FOR FASTING SUCCESS

Making meals that fit your fasting schedule is super easy. Keep it simple and packed with nutrients. Alright, let's get started with breakfast. Overnight oats with berries are awesome. Before hitting the hay, toss some rolled oats in a jar with almond milk, a sprinkle of cinnamon, and a handful of berries—fresh or frozen. Quite easy! By morning, you'll have a delicious, creamy meal loaded with fiber and antioxidants, ready to dig into! Craving something warm? Try steel-cut oats cooked in almond milk, topped with sliced bananas and walnuts for a cozy breakfast kickstart! Both recipes are straightforward to prepare in advance, giving you extra morning minutes and a healthy start to your day.

Thinking about lunch? How about a quinoa salad with chickpeas? Yum! It's a tasty and satisfying choice, packed with protein, fiber, and all the essential amino acids you need. Mix cooked quinoa, canned chickpeas, cherry tomatoes, and diced cucumber, then top with a sprinkle of feta cheese. Drizzle some olive oil and add a squeeze of lemon for a zesty dressing. This salad is delicious and versatile—just toss in whatever veggies you've on hand. Add some chili flakes for a spicy kick if you prefer a hot dish.

Click on the QR code in the back of this book in the Bonus section for the recipes!

MEAL PLANNING FOR BUSY LIFESTYLES

Picture this: you wake up every day clear on what's for breakfast, lunch, and dinner, no more scrambling for last-minute meal ideas. Meal planning brings a sense of order, especially when you're juggling intermittent fasting with a hectic lifestyle. Meal planning can seriously make fasting way easier. Cutting down on decision fatigue clears your mind for other stuff you need to tackle. Stop stressing over what to cook and just enjoy your meals and the whole experience instead. Additionally, planning keeps your nutrition on track throughout the week, allowing you to meet your dietary goals without last-minute chaos.

Taking some time each week to plan is key to nailing your meal prep. Why not set aside some time each weekend to plan your meals for the week? It'll make your life easier! Take this time to create a meal plan or calendar that outlines your daily food intake and corresponding meal times. This organized approach helps you view your weekly nutrition in a clear and easy-to-understand light, ensuring you cover a wide range of foods to reach your health objectives.

Having a visual plan of your meals provides an open view of your diet, allowing you to make changes as necessary. This discovery has the potential to transform meal planning from a cumbersome activity into a seamless part of your daily lifestyle. Being flexible is crucial for creating a meal plan that works for you. Life can throw curveballs, so having a meal plan can significantly reduce stress and save you time. Get ready to whip up some interchangeable meal parts that you can mix and match all week long.

Batch Cooking: A Time-Saving Strategy for Healthy, Stress-Free Meals

Want to level up your cooking game? **Batch cooking** is an innovative, time-saving strategy that involves preparing large quantities of food at once and storing it for meals throughout the week. It's ideal for busy individuals who want to eat healthy without the daily stress of cooking. At the start of each week, set aside some time to prepare large batches of staple foods, such as brown rice, quinoa, and barley, along with lean meats, tofu, legumes, and a variety of colorful vegetables. This smart move saves you time throughout the week. You'll have a wealth of healthy ingredients on hand, perfect for preparing a variety of delicious meals.

Storing your batch-cooked goodies in glass containers is recommended for several reasons. Firstly, glass is completely inert so that it won't interact with your food. That means your meals keep their original flavors without any weird taste transfers. Additionally, glass containers help keep your food fresh longer due to their airtight seals. They're super handy for reheating since they're safe for both the oven and microwave, making it a breeze to go from fridge to table. Additionally, opting for glass over plastic is a wise choice for the planet and helps you live a more sustainable life.

Batch cooking is super practical and fits perfectly with your intermittent fasting routine. Keeping a bunch of prepped ingredients ready makes it super easy to whip up meals that fit your eating schedule. Less time in the kitchen means more time enjoying your food. This method ensures that on your craziest days, you still get healthy meals that align with your fasting goals, keeping you on track with your health journey.

Batch cooking is also budget-friendly, as you are buying in bulk, and it reduces your overall grocery bill. Lastly, batch cooking reduces decision fatigue. No more stressing about "What's for Dinner", as all your meals have been predetermined and pre-portioned for the week. Thereby decreases your meal prep and cooking time exponentially.

Adding these meal prep tips to your routine will boost your fasting lifestyle and improve your overall health. With a bit of planning, eating healthy can be easy and fun, keeping both your body and mind happy and satisfied.

Simplify Your Routine with Digital Meal Planning Tools

Want to make meal planning easier? Explore various digital tools and resources. There are numerous apps available that make meal planning a breeze with customizable templates, recipe ideas, and handy shopping lists. Digital planners are a game-changer! They save you time and lighten the mental load of meal organizing, making it way more fun. Apps like Zero, DoFasting, and BodyFast offer fasting schedules and meal-planning tools that fit right into your daily life. Printable templates and shopping lists are super handy for anyone who likes to get their hands dirty. Sorting your shopping list by the store layout can streamline your grocery runs, helping you grab everything you need in one go.

Checklist: Meal Planning for Success

1. Set aside a dedicated time each week for meal planning.

2. Use a meal template or calendar to visualize your week.
3. Prepare interchangeable meal components for flexibility.
4. Keep staple ingredients stocked for quick meals.
5. Utilize digital planners or printable templates to streamline the process.

Use this checklist to seamlessly blend meal planning into your fasting routine, helping you stay organized and on track with your health goals.

GROCERY SHOPPING FOR A FASTING-FRIENDLY KITCHEN

You walk into your kitchen, you open the pantry wide, and voilà! It's stocked with all the ingredients you need to prepare a great meal. A well-stocked kitchen is pure magic. Having the necessary ingredients is like having a great toolkit; it makes cooking easier and more convenient when you're in a hurry. Stock your kitchen with whole grains, lean proteins, and a variety of fruits and vegetables. They are the foundation of a healthy diet and provide your body with the essential nutrients and energy it needs. Grab some brown rice, quinoa, chicken breasts, and a bunch of colorful veggies. These handy ingredients enable you to prepare a variety of dishes quickly. Keep healthy snacks handy during your meals. Nuts, seeds, and dried fruits are excellent picks. They provide a satisfying crunch and a nice energy boost without adding too many calories.

Fasting-Friendly Pantry Essentials: Beans, Nuts, Seeds & Dried Fruits

Let's dive into the must-haves for a fasting-friendly pantry, starting with the essential canned beans and legumes. These everyday staples aren't just easy to grab; they're packed with nutritional goodness. Beans and legumes are rich in protein and fiber, making them an excellent base for a variety of meals. They add a hearty texture that takes salads, soups, and stews to the next level. Creamy cannellini or robust black beans, each type packs its flavor and nutrition, making them kitchen MVPs.

Nuts and seeds are the hidden gems of snacks and meal toppings. Almonds, walnuts, chia seeds, and flaxseeds are rich in omega-3 fatty acids, which are beneficial for heart and brain health. They add a tasty crunch and extra flavor to everything from oatmeal and salads to yogurt and baked treats. Plus, their healthy fats help keep you full, which is super important for weight management, especially for women over 50.

Dried fruits like apricots, raisins, and figs pack a punch of energy and sweetness, making them an excellent go-to option for satisfying sugar cravings without refined sugar. They're fantastic in trail mixes, tossed on salads for a sweet kick, or even stewed up to add a tasty twist to savory meals. But please, watch out for that sugar! Enjoy them in moderation, and ensure they don't contain any added sugars or preservatives.

Adding these foods to your meals can boost their nutritional value. They offer a wide range of vitamins, minerals, and other key nutrients. These foods are great for your health and super versatile, making your meals both healthy and fun to prepare.

Cart Smart: Building a Fasting-Friendly Kitchen from the Aisles Up

Smart grocery shopping is essential for maintaining a fasting-friendly kitchen. Start by creating a shopping list that follows the store's layout. This strategy reduces aimless aisle wandering and keeps you focused on what you planned to buy. When selecting produce, opt for items that are in season. They're not just fresher; they're usually cheaper and way more flavorful, too. Seasonal shopping means you get to enjoy fruits and veggies when they're at their best, tasting great and packed with nutrients. Additionally, it spices up your diet, making meals more enjoyable and in tune with nature's rhythms.

Shopping on a budget doesn't have to mean skimping on quality. Buying in bulk is a smart move to save cash on essentials like grains, nuts, and spices. Check out sales or discounts on these items, and consider joining a wholesale club if you have the space for it. Buying organic is excellent, but opting for generic or store brands can save you a significant amount of money without sacrificing quality. Check prices and stay open to options to slash your grocery bill without sacrificing nutrition.

In your fabulous kitchen, as you prepare to cook your next meal, remember that every ingredient you select is a step toward better health and feeling great. These strategies aren't just about shopping; they're about creating a lifestyle that supports your fasting goals and boosts your energy. Your kitchen is your health companion, providing you with everything you need to prepare tasty, balanced meals.

As we move forward, we're exploring how to combine exercise with fasting. Let's explore how getting active enhances the benefits of what you eat! All these elements will boost your wellness and energy.

8

INTEGRATING EXERCISE WITH FASTING

As we age, staying active is crucial for our health. Moving your body, whether through exercise or just getting up and about, can only benefit your overall health. As a woman over 50, aging brings natural changes—slower metabolism, hormonal fluctuations, and loss of lean muscle. But when intermittent fasting (IF) is combined with smart exercise, it becomes a powerful strategy for burning stubborn fat, boosting energy & mental clarity, preserving muscle mass, and balancing hormones. This chapter presents exercise strategies and routines that are safe and effective to pair with intermittent fasting, allowing you to maximize the benefits of this approach.

EXERCISE ROUTINES FOR WOMEN OVER 50

Even though we may not have the strength or stamina we had in our 20s, there is no reason why we can't still push ourselves to be the strongest and fastest we can be. However, know your limits and choose workouts that match your fitness level. It's key to avoiding injury.

Finding Your Balance: High-Impact vs. Low-Impact Exercise After 50

There are two types of work: High-impact and Low-impact exercises. High-impact exercise is characterized by both feet leaving the ground simultaneously, creating greater force on the joints (especially the knees, hips, and ankles), such as running, jumping, or participating in aerobic workouts. High-impact exercise builds bone density, burns more calories in less time, and

boosts cardiovascular fitness. However, as a woman over 50, it can significantly stress your joints and increase the risk of injury if not done correctly or with good form. Instead, consider low-impact exercises. This type of exercise involves keeping at least one foot on the ground at all times. It is ideal for beginners and older adults by minimizing stress on your joints, leading to fewer injuries, while also improving strength, flexibility, and cardiovascular health. Some examples of low-impact exercises are water aerobics, swimming, walking, and biking. They provide a full-body workout while being gentle on your joints. The water lifts you, making these exercises perfect for anyone with joint issues or arthritis. Stationary biking is also a great low-impact option. You can crank up the intensity while boosting your heart health. Walking is also a great low-impact exercise that can be done anywhere, anytime, with no equipment needed. All these activities are gentle on your body and highly energizing, offering a welcome respite from the daily grind. Additionally, they're highly adaptable for any fitness level, allowing you to adjust the intensity to match your needs and energy levels during fasting.

Consistency in your exercise routine is key. Sticking to a regular workout routine helps keep your joints healthy and mobile, which is crucial for staying active as you age. Regularly moving around keeps your joints well-lubricated, which helps reduce stiffness and improve flexibility. It boosts your heart health and keeps your circulation in top shape. This mix of perks makes life more lively and enjoyable, allowing you to appreciate the things you love truly. Moreover, working out is great for your mental health, as it helps reduce stress and boost your mood. Getting active boosts endorphins, lifting your mood, and naturally fighting off the blues.

Finding time to exercise in a packed schedule might seem like a challenge, but with a bit of planning, you can easily make it happen. Set aside specific times for exercise and treat them like essential appointments you can't skip. Pick times that work with your energy and daily schedule—whether it's a morning walk, an afternoon yoga class, or a chill evening swim. Quick, regular workouts can pack a punch just as effectively as longer ones, especially when you're short on time. A quick 10-minute brisk walk or some bodyweight exercises can have a significant impact. Find ways to incorporate movement into your day, such as taking the stairs instead of the elevator or parking a bit farther from the store entrance.

REFLECTION EXERCISE: CREATING YOUR EXERCISE PLAN

Think about your exercise routine and how it will mesh with your fasting pattern. Think about what you enjoy doing and at what time of day you are most energetic. Develop a simple weekly exercise routine that incorporates cardio, weight training, and flexibility, tailored to your individual needs. Be flexible and be yourself, accepting modifications based on what you want to do each day. This routine is your ticket to a healthier, more energetic life.

The pairing of fasting and exercise offers a holistic approach to improving your overall health, body, and mind. As you are caught up in the euphoria of motion, remain attuned to the signals your body is sending; recognize its cues and revel in the power it has to give.

STRENGTH TRAINING AND FASTING: BUILDING MUSCLE

Resistance training, also known as strength training, is essential for women over 50. Resistance training involves working your muscles against resistance, such as:

- Dumbbells, resistance bands, or kettlebells
- Bodyweight (squats, push-ups, planks)
- Machines or functional movements (e.g., step-ups, wall sits)

Pairing strength training with intermittent fasting can supercharge your results, helping you burn fat, build lean muscle, and protect your metabolism as you age. As we age, our bodies naturally begin to lose muscle mass due to a decline in growth hormone, a sedentary lifestyle, inadequate protein intake, and insulin resistance. A condition known as sarcopenia. This decline in muscle mass increases your risk of falls and fractures. It slows your metabolism, making weight gain and insulin resistance more likely. It can also lead to frailty, loss of independence, and decreased quality of life, making even basic daily tasks more challenging to manage. However, strength training is a powerful way to combat sarcopenia. By regularly engaging in strength exercises, you can prevent or slow down muscle loss, maintaining your body's strength and agility. Aim for 2-4 sessions per week, focusing on the major muscle groups, upper, lower, and core. The main upper body exercises include the back, shoulders, and arms. The primary lower body exercises target the glutes, quadriceps, hamstrings, and calves. Main core exercises include the abdominal muscles and lower back.

Building muscle does more than just keep you toned; it significantly boosts your metabolism. Your metabolism kicks into high gear, burning more calories even when you're just relaxing. This helps with weight management and increases your overall energy levels. This boost in metabolism gives you the energy to dive into your favorite activities, making life a lot more enjoyable.

The Power Duo: Intermittent Fasting and Strength Training for Maximum Results

Intermittent fasting and strength training work together to significantly enhance your fitness results, as fasting increases growth hormone levels, which are crucial for building and repairing muscles. Pretty cool, right? Fasting also encourages fat-burning, while strength training signals the body to hold onto muscle, even in a calorie deficit. Fasting activates autophagy (cellular cleanup), while strength training stimulates muscle regeneration—a powerful anti-aging combo. Lastly, this combo lowers insulin resistance, which means better blood sugar control and easier fat loss, especially around the belly.

Timing your strength training workout to coincide with your fasting schedule can help maximize your results. If you train before your first meal, the benefits include burning fat, boosting mental clarity, and improving hormonal balance. Suppose you train after breaking your fast. In that case, lifting heavier weights will produce better performance and muscle growth. Eating protein-packed foods immediately after a workout provides your muscles with the boost they need to repair and grow. This innovative approach ensures your body gets the nutrients it needs to recover and significantly boost your strength training results.

If you're just starting with strength training or want to adjust your routine, begin with resistance training using bands and light weights. They're a great way to ease into strength training while still providing a solid challenge. Squats and lunges hit multiple muscle groups, making your workouts way more efficient and effective. These exercises enhance strength, balance, and coordination, which are crucial for maintaining physical fitness as we age. Focusing on these basic movements sets you up for a strong, resilient body that can tackle everyday challenges with ease.

Strength Training Safely While Fasting: Form, Balance, and Recovery

Safety comes first when it comes to strength training, particularly with fasting. Employ light resistance, gradually increasing it as you grow stronger. This approach minimizes the risk of injury, enabling your body to adapt slowly to the demands of strength training. Ensure proper form and technique, as incorrect form may result in sprains or strains. Try working with a fitness professional or looking online to learn the form of every exercise. Don't forget to warm up and cool down; it's very significant. Warming up prepares your joints and muscles for use, making injuries less likely. Cooling down allows your body to return to a resting state, thereby enhancing recovery and flexibility.

Pay attention to your body and listen to what it's telling you while you're hitting the weights. Some days, you just feel more pumped than others. Vary your workouts and ensure you include rest and recovery time when needed. Finding this balance is crucial for maintaining your fitness routine while fasting. It's all about discovering a routine that aligns with your lifestyle, supports your health goals, and helps you live life to the fullest.

CARDIOVASCULAR HEALTH: WALKING AND LIGHT CARDIO

Cardio is essential for maintaining your heart's health, especially as you age. Regular cardio helps your heart and lungs function more efficiently, making each beat and breath count. With this boost in efficiency, your heart gets a break, which in turn lowers the chances of heart disease and other related health issues. Cardio helps with weight management and fat loss, especially when paired with intermittent fasting. When you get your heart pumping during a workout, your body burns more calories, making it easier to shed those extra pounds and maintain a healthy weight.

Walking is one of the easiest and most accessible ways to get some exercise. It's gentle on the body, making it perfect for everyone while still providing a solid workout. Walking is excellent, whether you're strolling around your neighborhood, taking a walk in the park, or hitting the treadmill at the gym. It's easy on your joints and packed with benefits. It's an excellent opportunity to socialize—grab some friends or join a local walking group. This adds a fun social twist to your routine, making it way more enjoyable and giving you that extra push to stay active.

Light cardio is excellent for maintaining your heart health without depleting your energy, especially on fasting days. Quick walks after meals can significantly aid digestion and help keep your metabolism active. Light cycling workouts are an excellent option, be it pedaling along on a stationary bicycle or riding through the great outdoors. These activities raise your heart rate high enough to enhance your cardiovascular health without draining your energy levels while fasting. You can remain active and involved without depleting your energy, achieving the benefits of exercise while adhering to your fasting principles.

Making cardio an enjoyable, low-maintenance activity is key to maintaining a consistent routine. Taking a walk through nature reserves or finding local parks can make a simple walk an exciting experience, providing a change of environment and some fresh air to boot. Getting outdoors can completely transform your workout, turning it from a dreaded task into an exciting getaway. Listening to music or podcasts can enhance your experience, keeping your mind both stimulated and entertained as you go about your journey. Whether you choose an upbeat playlist or a gripping podcast, these audio companions can turn your cardio sessions into a pleasurable and laid-back experience.

YOGA AND STRETCHING: ENHANCING FLEXIBILITY AND BALANCE

Picture this: you wake up every morning feeling flexible and in sync, your body gliding effortlessly through the day. Yoga and stretching can significantly deliver on this promise, especially for women over 50. As we age, staying flexible is extremely important. Our joints and muscles can become tight, leading to stiffness and discomfort. Yoga is a great way to unwind. Yoga boosts joint flexibility and range of motion, keeping us agile and our movements smooth. It's not just about bending and posing; it's about feeling totally at ease in your skin with limbs that move just right.

Yoga isn't just about getting fit; it also calms your mind. It promotes mindful breathing and meditation, transforming your space into a serene zone away from daily chaos. This practice helps reduce stress and promote relaxation, making it an ideal complement to the fasting lifestyle. Yoga lowers cortisol, your body's primary stress hormone, through a combination of physical movement, breath control, mind-fulness, and relaxation, all of which directly influence your nervous system and hormonal balance. It aids digestion and detoxification, making it easier for your body to absorb nutrients during meals. This holistic approach enhances both body and mind, fostering a sense of well-being that permeates every aspect of life.

It is easy to fit yoga into your life. Choose a consistent time frame, be it a peaceful morning or a night of tranquility. Doing it habitually makes it less of a task and more of a cherished ritual. Seek out local classes or jump into online courses to benefit from professional guidance and build a community. These tools offer intense sequences and expert advice to enhance your practice and keep you motivated. Yoga is about progression, not perfection, so enjoy the process along the way. With a commitment to practice, you will probably notice improvements in your flexibility, balance, and overall health.

Want to make yoga a regular part of your life? Set up a special spot at home just for your practice. No need to go overboard—just find a calm place with a mat and some calming stuff like candles or plants, and you're good to go. A specific spot can help you get in the zone for practice, letting your mind and body know it's time to focus and relax. Also, pay attention to your body and respect its limits. Some days, you'll feel super flexible and full of energy, while on other days, you might need a gentler approach. Roll with the ups and downs and tweak your practice as needed.

As we conclude this chapter on combining exercise with fasting, it's clear that staying active is crucial for boosting health and energy. Strength training helps increase and maintain muscle, which in turn aids in stability and balance. While Cardio exercise helps with weight loss, yoga is excellent for improving flexibility and balance. They team up for a comprehensive approach to well-being, taking care of both body and mind. As we move forward, let's explore the social and emotional aspects of fasting and examine how this lifestyle shift can enhance our relationships and mental well-being.

9

SOCIAL AND EMOTIONAL
ASPECTS OF FASTING

E very year, I host an annual summer party to celebrate the 4th
of July. Friends and family gather together, laughing and chatting, while drinks and snacks flow freely. This past summer
was the first time I hosted an event while fasting. So there I was, caught
in a silent struggle, trying to stick to my fasting goals while resisting all
those delicious, high-calorie foods and drinks. Understandably, social
events can be tricky when you're trying to stick to intermittent fasting.
You sometimes feel the pressure and temptation to throw caution to
the wind and simply eat what looks good. You might also feel left out
while trying to enjoy socializing and sticking to your health goals.

Attending social events while fasting can still be a pleasant experience.
Plan ahead, and you can stick to your fasting routine without missing
out on the fun. One smart move is to time your fasting and eating
windows with social events. If you know a meal-focused event is
coming up, adjust your eating schedule accordingly. You can join in on
the fun and still stick to your fasting plan. Another way is to politely
decline food offers without feeling awkward. Just say, "I'm not hungry
right now, but thanks." That usually works. People will respect your

choices, especially when you keep your reasons straightforward and upbeat.

Engaging in non-food activities can completely lighten the atmosphere at social gatherings. Jump into conversations and networking, soaking up the stories and laughs all around you. Real connections happen way beyond the buffet line. Participate in activities like dancing or games, which let you soak up the fun without food stealing the spotlight. These activities are both fun and entertaining, making your experience even more enjoyable. Shifting the focus from food to interaction can significantly enhance the fun and satisfaction at social events.

Being clear about your fasting habits is crucial for handling social situations smoothly. When the topic arises, share your story in a way that resonates with your friends.

- Fasting has seriously boosted my health.
- I've got way more energy, and my mental clarity is on point.
- It's like a reset button for my body and mind.

Keep it simple and avoid getting bogged down in complicated stuff that could confuse people. Focus on the benefits and changes you've noticed in your body. This approach not only shares knowledge but also sparks curiosity and respect. It may even inspire others to adopt healthier habits.

REFLECTION EXERCISE: PLANNING YOUR NEXT SOCIAL EVENT

Consider an upcoming social gathering you plan to attend. Grab a notepad or journal and start writing down any challenges you might face, along with how you plan to tackle them. Consider your fasting window and how it aligns with the event's schedule. Reflect on your social experiences and identify the strategies that truly resonated with you. Planning can significantly boost your confidence and enable you to enjoy the event while adhering to your fasting goals.

These strategies can change your perspective on how you view food and social gatherings. It's all about figuring out what works for you and being prepared to adapt. You'll find that sticking to your fasting goals doesn't mean you have to skip out on social fun. It's all about finding that sweet spot between staying healthy and enjoying your social life. Remember that every event is an opportunity to refine your fasting skills and connect with others. Over time, you'll notice that social events become easier, allowing you to have fun with others while still sticking to your health goals.

BUILDING A SUPPORT NETWORK FOR YOUR FASTING JOURNEY

Starting intermittent fasting can be like navigating through unfamiliar waters. Having a supportive group is like having a lighthouse to guide you through the ups and downs of fasting. Posting about it on social media can honestly change the game on those tough days. On days when there are just too many temptations, it is an absolute lifesaver to have someone to hold you accountable. Having fellow fasters in your corner can be quite beneficial in helping you stay on track with your fast. They truly grasp the ins and outs of fasting, demonstrating a genuine understanding and care. Hearing stories and tips from people who have gone through similar experiences can put your mind at ease. It's great to see that others have faced similar challenges and found effective ways to tackle them.

Building a supportive community can be pretty straightforward. Look for local fasting groups or online forums to meet others who share your interests. These places are goldmines of info, packed with folks ready to share their insights and stories. Fasting workshops and seminars are an excellent way to connect with others and explore the nuances of fasting practices in depth. Here, you can chat about strategies, celebrate wins, and even make friends who go beyond just fasting. Joining a Meetup group for intermittent fasting can connect you with a group of supportive individuals who understand your goals. These groups are composed of numerous diverse individuals, each bringing their own unique insights and helpful tips.

Your family and friends are crucial to your support system. Their involvement can significantly enhance your fasting experience. Get them involved in some fasting-friendly fun. Go for a walk together or whip up a new healthy recipe together. Doing things together really amps up your commitment. It fosters stronger relationships, enabling everyone to understand better and respect your health goals. They might help with meal planning, whip up dishes that match your fasting routine, or even give fasting a shot themselves.

My friend Gina crushed it when her husband jumped on board with her fasting journey. They began whipping up meals together and chatting about their progress, which brought them closer as a couple and kept the motivation flowing.

Another connection made was between Jane and her fasting partner, Lisa. They met at a local fasting seminar and instantly became each other's rock. They often connect, swap meal ideas, and pump each other up when things get tough. Their teamwork has been key to their success.

I joined a fasting group at my local gym. Everyone had their own goals, but they came together and celebrated every win as a team. Everyone had each other's backs, creating an environment where we all felt motivated to push beyond our limits. This challenge made me feel like I belonged and kept me motivated to stay on track.

Creating a support network means being open and ready to connect with people. It's all about building connections that strengthen your determination and enhance your fasting journey. Having a support network, whether it's local groups, online communities, or friends and family, can turn fasting from a lonely task into a fun group adventure.

FASTING AND FAMILY: BALANCING SOCIAL LIFE AND HEALTH GOALS

Think about the warm, familiar smell of a family recipe wafting through the house or a dish that has been shared for generations, packed with memories of good times and love. Family meals aren't just about the food; they're a classic time to share stories and strengthen those bonds. Introducing fasting can feel like trying to fit a square peg into a round hole. Meal timing and preferences can cause some tension. Perhaps you decided to skip breakfast, but the rest of the family starts the day with a big meal together. Or maybe your fasting window wraps up right when they're about to dig into dinner. Timing issues can throw you off, making it feel like you're on a totally different schedule than everyone else. Family traditions centered around food, such as Sunday brunches or holiday feasts, can be especially challenging. You may find yourself torn between enjoying these special moments and adhering to your fasting routine.

Fasting With Family: Creating Support and Balance

Balancing fasting with family life is doable and can be super rewarding. Try syncing your fasting windows with family meals for a practical solution. If your family usually eats dinner at 7 PM, consider adjusting your eating window to allow for a meal together. A minor tweak can really help keep everyone on the same page while you stick to your health goals. Making fasting-friendly meals that everyone in the family will love is a great way to connect. Load up on whole foods, such as vegetables, lean proteins, and healthy fats, to satisfy everyone's dietary needs. Involving your family in meal planning can lead to tasty and nutritious dishes that everyone will love, ensuring no one feels left out.

Getting your family involved in fasting activities can create a supportive mood. Host a potluck where everyone brings a dish that aligns with your fasting preferences. Introducing your family to new foods and recipes can be a blast and get everyone chatting about healthy eating. Teaching your family about the perks of fasting can be an eye-opening experience. Talk about how fasting has boosted your energy, lifted your mood, or made you feel healthier. Invite others to join you in checking out these perks. They might surprise you with how willing they are to try something new, especially when they notice the positive changes in you. Sharing this experience can boost your dedication to fasting and tighten your family ties.

Keeping the lines of communication open with family is key to a smooth fasting experience. Be clear about meal times and get their help with your fasting goals. Ensure they understand the significant benefits this commitment will bring to their health and well-being, and invite them to share any questions or concerns they may have. Open communication regarding these matters can clarify misunderstandings and provide a healthier atmosphere. Acknowledge the challenge they are having with their new routine and look for ways to reach a compromise. They might help by picking restaurants with good fasting options or even giving fasting a shot themselves. Having mutual understanding and respect can make your fasting journey feel less lonely and more like a fun adventure together.

Fasting with family can be challenging, but with patience, flexibility, and adaptability, it can be made to work. It's all about striking a balance between your health goals and the family traditions that mean the most to you. Get your family involved in your fasting routine and keep the conversation flowing. This way, you'll create a supportive atmosphere that enhances your fasting commitment while enjoying quality time with your family. Finding that balance takes time and effort, but it can lead to a more enjoyable experience for everyone. Keep in mind that having your family's support can boost your fasting journey and help you improve both your health and relationships.

MINDFUL EATING PRACTICES: CULTIVATING A HEALTHY RELATIONSHIP WITH FOOD

Mindful eating is the practice of bringing full attention and awareness to your eating experience—what you eat, how you eat, and why you eat. It helps you build a better relationship with food, recognize hunger and fullness cues, and enjoy meals without guilt or distraction. It's all about tuning into your body's hunger and fullness signals, which can easily get overlooked in our busy lives. Paying attention to these signals can help you recognize when to splurge and when to set the fork aside, keeping your meal on track. In this manner, you will be able to maximize the textures and flavors in each morsel, making meals so much more pleasurable. Imagine biting into a crisp apple or inhaling the aroma of a home-cooked meal. Being attentive makes eating a fun, mindful experience instead of just a quick chore.

Core Principles of Mindful Eating

Eat with awareness

- Focus on the taste, texture, smell, and appearance of food.
- Eat slowly and without distractions, such as phones or TV.

Listen to your body

- Pause before eating and ask yourself, "*Am I truly hungry, or am I bored, stressed, or tired?*" Stop eating when comfortably full, not stuffed.

Remove judgment

- Avoid labeling foods as "good" or "bad."
- Allow all foods in moderation without shame.

Use all your senses

- Notice how the food looks, smells, sounds (crunchy?), and tastes.
- Savor every bite.

Gratitude and intention

- Take a moment to appreciate your food.
- Acknowledge its origin and how it nourishes your body.

Mindful eating can significantly aid our fasting game by helping you focus on quality instead of just piling on the food during your eating windows. It encourages you to choose your foods more carefully and be intentional, which helps reduce overeating. Mindful eating helps you feel full and happy with smaller portions. As you start to notice the different flavors and textures, meals become way more fun and satisfying. Feeling satisfied can help you avoid overeating since you're more in tune with your body's hunger cues. Focusing on the eating experience enables you to develop healthier habits that align with your fasting goals and foster a better relationship with food.

Simple Tips to Start Mindful Eating

- Start meals with a few sips of water and a moment of gratitude
- Take three deep breaths before eating
- Chew thoroughly (aim for 20–30 chews per bite)
- Put your fork down between bites
- Eat without screens—just you and your food

Take a moment for a quick pre-meal meditation or try some deep breathing to clear your mind and prepare for the food to come your way. Try slowing down and truly savoring each bite to bring mindfulness to your eating habits. Chew your food thoroughly and savor the taste and texture of each bite. This helps with digestion, allowing you to enjoy every meal truly. Cutting out distractions like TV or phones while eating can help you focus on your food. Create a relaxing atmosphere for your meals, where you can savor your food without any distractions. This practice enables you to stay present and truly connect with your food. It's all about making mealtime special and appreciating the food and the energy it gives us.

Enhance your mindful eating by incorporating exercises that help you stay present and focused.

These tips can help you enjoy your meals more, making you feel calm and thankful for the food you get. Journaling about your food experiences and feelings can be super helpful. After each meal, take a moment to reflect on how you felt before, during, and after eating. This exercise helps you identify patterns in your eating habits, such as emotional triggers that lead to overeating or foods that either boost or drain your energy.

Mindful eating is not about following strict rules, but rather about savoring the enjoyment of your food. It is about savoring each bite and making the whole experience something meaningful and enjoyable. As you tune into your body and make thoughtful food choices, you can cultivate a healthier relationship with food that leads to better overall well-being. This practice beautifully complements intermittent fasting by emphasizing the importance of nutritious food and paying attention to your body's signals. The adoption of mindful eating can elevate your fasting experience to the next level and transform your approach to nutrition and health.

10

OVERCOMING CHALLENGES AND COMMON OBJECTIONS

You're in your cozy kitchen on a chilly, rainy afternoon, surrounded by the heavenly smell of fresh coffee. Yet your thoughts drift to the pantry, where cookies and chips, those delicious little goodies, call your name, particularly when life gets the better of you. During fasting, hunger and craving strike ruthlessly, weakening your resolve. It's not just your stomach growling; it's that emotional hunger that kicks in when you're stressed, anxious, or just plain bored. Getting a grip on these triggers is a big part of the struggle, and it's something a lot of women deal with, especially when fasting is in the mix. Emotional stress can be a sneaky little monster, prompting you to reach for food as a form of comfort. Anxiety can ramp up those hunger pangs, making it a cycle where food feels like a quick fix but doesn't solve anything. Then there's boredom, and suddenly eating turns into a go-to move to fill that space.

MASTERING CRAVINGS: HYDRATION, SMART FOOD CHOICES, AND MINDSET

Dealing with cravings requires a well-planned approach that focuses on your mindset and taking effective action.

Staying Hydrated: The Secret Weapon for Successful Fasting

Staying hydrated is *crucial* for a safe and effective fasting experience. When you fast, your body naturally shifts into a state where it uses stored energy (like fat) for fuel. During this process, the body sheds water and electrolytes as insulin levels drop. This can lead to dehydration, which may cause symptoms like headaches, fatigue, brain fog, dizziness, and muscle cramps, especially in women over 50, who may already experience hormonal shifts that affect fluid balance.

Combining fasting with *clever hydration techniques* is crucial for managing hunger and maintaining steady energy levels. Aim to drink at least half of your body weight in ounces of water daily, or more if you're physically active.

Incorporating **herbal teas** such as chamomile, ginger, or peppermint adds both flavor and function. Chamomile has calming properties that can help reduce stress-related cravings. Ginger tea supports digestion and can soothe an unsettled stomach during more extended fasting periods. Peppermint tea is refreshing and has been shown to help suppress appetite naturally.

Black coffee, when consumed in moderation, can also be an effective tool. The caffeine provides a mild appetite-suppressing effect and boosts mental focus during fasting windows. It may also gently stimulate metabolism, making it easier to sustain energy levels. However, stick to plain black coffee without cream or sugar to keep your fast intact, and avoid overconsumption to prevent dehydration or jitters.

For an extra boost, consider adding a pinch of **electrolytes or mineral salt** to your water, especially if you are doing extended fasting or sweating through exercise. Maintaining electrolyte balance helps prevent headaches, fatigue, and cravings caused by mineral loss.

The key is to make hydration part of your fasting routine, turning it into a ritual. Keeping a water bottle or thermos of herbal tea handy creates a sense of comfort, keeps your hands busy, and helps you ride out hunger waves while nourishing your body in a fast-friendly way.

How Hydration Supports Your Body

- Flushes out toxins and cellular waste released during fat breakdown and autophagy (the body's natural "cleanup" process during fasting).
- Regulates body temperature and prevents the chills that some women experience while fasting.
- Supports kidney function and prevents constipation, a common issue that can occur when dietary intake is reduced.
- Alleviates cravings—thirst is often mistaken for hunger.
- Maintaining electrolyte balance is vital for heart, brain, and muscle function.

Remember, fasting isn't about deprivation. It's about making space for healing and growth. Water is one critical part of that equation.

Preventing Cravings With High-Fiber Foods and Mindful Eating

The best way to overcome cravings is to stop them before they start, and one of the most effective strategies is focusing on what you eat during your eating windows. **High-fiber foods** are your secret weapon because they keep you feeling full longer and help stabilize blood sugar levels, which can reduce those sudden hunger spikes. Foods like oats, beans, lentils, and a variety of colorful vegetables create bulk in the digestive system, slowing the absorption of glucose and providing steady, sustained energy throughout the day.

Soluble fiber, found in foods such as oats and beans, forms a gel-like substance in the gut that promotes satiety and supports gut health, while insoluble fiber from veggies and whole grains aids in digestion and keeps things moving smoothly. This combination not only helps you stay fuller but also supports a healthy gut microbiome, which can influence hunger hormones and cravings.

Pairing high-fiber foods with **lean protein and healthy fats** during meals can further enhance satiety and provide a balanced nutrient profile that keeps your metabolism humming. By fueling your body with nutrient-dense, high-fiber meals, you're not only curbing cravings but also giving yourself the foundation for steady energy, balanced mood, and long-term fasting success.

Harnessing a Positive Mindset to Conquer Cravings

Your mindset is one of the most powerful tools in managing cravings during fasting. Approaching hunger with a **positive perspective** can shift how you experience it. Instead of seeing it as an enemy, view hunger as a natural signal from your body, a gentle reminder of your internal rhythms and metabolic processes. This shift in thinking reduces stress and makes fasting feel more intentional and empowering.

Mindful distraction is another effective strategy. Engaging in activities that keep both your mind and hands occupied, like reading a good book, tending to your garden, journaling, or working on a puzzle, can redirect your focus and help cravings pass. Physical activities such as light stretching or a short walk can also help reset your mental state while supporting your overall health.

Always keep the **bigger picture** in mind: every craving you resist is a step closer to your health and wellness goals. Visualizing the benefits of fasting, such as better energy, weight balance, and improved longevity, can reinforce your motivation in those challenging moments. Each time you successfully ride out a craving, you're not just avoiding a snack; you're strengthening your discipline and commitment to feeling vibrant, balanced, and healthy.

Linda, a lively woman in her 50s, constantly struggled to fight off cravings while fasting. She started using distraction techniques, such as taking quick walks whenever a craving struck. Eventually, she realized her cravings were fading, and those walks helped keep her hunger in check and boosted her mood.

Nancy's got an inspiring story about her battle with late-night snacking. After tweaking her eating habits and adding more fiber-packed foods to her dinner, she noticed her late-night cravings fading away. She didn't just beat hunger; she took charge of her eating habits, boosting her empowerment and confidence.

REFLECTION EXERCISE: IDENTIFYING YOUR TRIGGERS

Why not try keeping a hunger diary for a week? It could be an eye-opening experience. Pay attention to when cravings strike, what sparks them, and how you react. Do certain times of day or feelings make cravings hit harder? This diary helps you track your hunger patterns and develop personalized strategies to manage them more effectively. Figuring out your triggers is the first step to mastering them so you can enjoy fasting without those pesky cravings pulling at you.

FASTING WITH PRE-EXISTING MEDICAL CONDITIONS

When addressing intermittent fasting, particularly if you have ongoing health concerns, it is best to proceed with caution and deliberation. Just as embarking on a journey without a map is foolish, starting a new health regimen needs to be a well-strategized endeavor. Always begin by consulting a medical professional. They will assist in designing a personalized fasting program tailored to your specific health needs, with utmost care. Your doctor can help you determine how fasting may affect your medication or current health status. When you are dealing with diabetes, thyroid, or other conditions, a professional will help you determine the best course of action.

For individuals managing diabetes, adjusting your fasting schedule is also crucial. Fasting does make insulin more sensitive, but you must still monitor it closely. Monitoring your blood glucose level ensures that it remains stable and safe during your fasting period. Shorter fasting periods may be the most beneficial, allowing you to maintain your energy levels without worrying about a crash. If thyroid issues are your concern, some adjustments are also necessary. Fasting may be beneficial for individuals with specific thyroid issues; however, others should proceed with caution. It is reasonable to begin by tailoring your fasting program to suit the particular needs of your body. You may start with less severe fasting techniques and intensify their severity as you gain strength and confidence.

Keeping a close eye on things is key to handling medical conditions effectively. Keeping an eye on blood sugar levels can help you dodge those sudden drops or spikes. Continuous glucose monitors provide real-time data, allowing you to adjust your fasting routine as needed. If you're dealing with chronic fatigue or experiencing fluctuations in your energy levels, shorter fasting periods may be the most effective approach. These changes make sure fasting boosts your health rather than putting it at risk. Pay attention to your body's signals and team up with a healthcare professional to safely incorporate fasting into your routine so you reap the benefits without the risks.

Fasting is not a one-size-fits-all approach, particularly when you have a pre-existing condition. Every individual is unique, with their own set of needs and responses. Customizing your fasting routine with the guidance of a healthcare provider enables you to reap the benefits of fasting without any issues. The key is finding what is best for you, making adjustments as needed along the way, and being willing to adapt. Intermittent fasting can potentially enhance your health practice and improve your quality of life, all while taking into account your medical needs.

AVOIDING MUSCLE LOSS: NUTRITION AND EXERCISE IN FASTING

Maintaining strong muscles is crucial, especially as we age. Muscles aren't just about looking strong or fit; they keep our metabolism going, boost joint health, and improve overall well-being. As we have learned, the risk of sarcopenia increases as we age. Strong muscles support your joints and bones, improving your posture, balance, and overall mobility, allowing you to move freely and confidently. Essential for independent living and reducing the risk of falls in older adults. That's why it's very important to keep your muscles strong, especially when you're fasting.

Your best defence to maintain or enhance your muscle health and enjoy the perks of intermittent fasting is nutrition. Ensure you focus on consuming enough protein at each meal. Protein is key for building muscles, and getting enough helps repair and grow muscle tissue. Be sure to include a protein source in every meal, such as lean meats, fish, eggs, beans, or dairy products.

Branch-Chain Amino Acids

Additionally, incorporating branched-chain amino acids (BCAAs) is crucial for building muscle protein. BCAAs are a group of three essential amino acids: **Leucine, Isoleucine, and Valine.** They're called *branched-chain* because of their unique chemical structure, and they're classified as essential because your body can't produce them. You must get them from food or supplements. You can get these essential amino acids from natural sources like meat, poultry, fish, eggs, dairy, whey protein, soy, and legumes. Or you can get them through supplements. Available in powder or capsule form, it is often taken during workouts or periods of fasting.

Exercise to Maintain Strong Muscles

We have also learned that exercising is an excellent way to maintain strong muscles. You must include resistance training in your routine. This type of workout fights against resistance to boost strength and is super effective at preserving muscle. Weightlifting, resistance bands, and bodyweight exercises, such as push-ups and squats, are excellent ways to enhance your muscle strength. Additionally, incorporate flexibility and balance workouts like Yoga and tai chi are excellent for enhancing muscle function and reducing the risk of falls.

Fitness professionals consistently emphasize the importance of planning your workouts around your fasting periods. Experiment with different approaches to find what works best for you and your life. Whatever you choose, just make sure your body gets enough time to recover. Rest is just as crucial as the workout. Getting enough sleep and staying hydrated are super important for recovery. They help fix your muscles and boost your energy levels.

Combining nutrition and exercise sets you up for optimal muscle health and allows you to enjoy the benefits of intermittent fasting. It's all about finding that sweet spot that works for you and your life.

Flexibility in Fasting: Adapting to Your Unique Needs

Think of your fasting schedule like a dance that grooves with your life, adjusting to your beat and vibe. Flexibility is what turns fasting from a strict routine into a manageable lifestyle you can stick with. It's all about fitting fasting into your daily routine, so it enhances your life instead of throwing it off balance. If you hit the gym early, consider eating right afterward to refuel your energy. If your evenings are packed with family dinners, pushing your eating window later lets you enjoy those moments without skipping a beat. This flexibility makes it easier to stick with fasting, turning it into a natural part of your routine instead of a hassle.

Carol's Story: How One Simple Shift Made Fasting Feel Effortless

Carol had been excited to try intermittent fasting after hearing about its benefits, including improved energy and easier weight management. But after a few weeks, she found herself struggling. The biggest challenge? Her fasting window ended hours before her family sat down for dinner.

Every evening, she faced the same dilemma: sit with her family and sip water while they enjoyed a warm meal, or break her fast and feel like she was "failing." It left her feeling isolated, frustrated, and disconnected from the people she loved most. Instead of giving up, Carol made a small but powerful change: she **adjusted her eating window** to begin later in the day and end just after dinner time. That simple shift changed everything.

Now, she shares family dinners with joy and ease, without guilt or stress. Fasting no longer feels like a burden. It fits seamlessly into her life rather than disrupting it. Carol not only feels more relaxed and connected at mealtime, but she's also more committed to her fasting lifestyle than ever before. That one tweak helped turn fasting into a habit she could truly sustain.

Tina's Story: Aligning Fasting with His Active Lifestyle

Tina has always been a morning person. By 6 a.m., she's out the door and on the trails, breathing in the crisp morning air and soaking in the stillness that only early hikes can offer. For her, these hikes aren't just exercise; they're a sacred ritual, a way to reset before the day begins.

When Tina first started intermittent fasting, he followed a typical 12-hour eating window from 12 pm to 8 pm. But something felt off. She began noticing that she was dragging through the morning, especially during her hikes. She'd return home hungry, depleted, and sometimes even lightheaded, precisely the opposite of how she wanted to feel.

Instead of abandoning fasting altogether, Tina decided to **shift her eating window earlier** to support her lifestyle. Now, she breaks her fast shortly after finishing her morning hike, giving her body the fuel it needs to recover and thrive. The difference was immediate and dramatic: she had more energy, a better mood, and an even stronger performance during her hikes.

What started as a struggle became a sustainable, energizing routine. For Tina, fasting is no longer something she "works around"; it now works with her, seamlessly fitting into hier rhythm and enhancing her well-being.

Her story is a powerful reminder: **flexibility is key**. When you tailor your fasting window to your lifestyle, not the other way around, fasting becomes not just doable but deeply rewarding.

Sabrina's Story: Finding Her Fasting Flow in a Hectic Life

Sabrina's calendar was always full. Between back-to-back work meetings, client lunches, and happy hours with friends, she felt like she was constantly on the go. When she first started intermittent fasting, she tried the classic 16:8 schedule—eating from noon to 8 p.m.—but it clashed with her daily routine.

Her mornings were fueled by black coffee and stress, and she often had to decline lunch invitations or sit awkwardly sipping water while everyone else ordered food. It made her feel restricted, not empowered. And by the end of the day, she found herself ravenous, eating whatever was quick and convenient instead of nourishing.

Ready to give up, Sabrina paused and asked herself an important question: *What would this look like if it actually worked for me?*

That's when she had her breakthrough. Instead of rigidly sticking to someone else's fasting plan, she **restructured her eating window** from 10 a.m. to 6 p.m.—giving her time to enjoy lunch meetings without pressure and still make early evening social events work.

The change was instant. Sabrina's energy improved, her meals felt intentional, and she stopped feeling like she had to choose between her health goals and her social life. Most importantly, fasting no longer felt like a burden—it felt liberating.

Now, Sabrina is thriving. She's more in tune with her body, more focused during the workday, and still fully present for the people and moments that matter most. Her story proves that success with fasting doesn't come from being perfect—it comes from being flexible.

When you embrace adaptability, fasting can be a great ally in your health and wellness journey. Experimenting with various schedules and routines allows you to discover what works best for your body and lifestyle. You can easily adjust your fasting schedule to fit your hectic work life or even make it a family affair; there are numerous options. This flexibility makes fasting more enjoyable and puts you in control of your health with ease.

OVERCOMING EMOTIONAL AND MENTAL BARRIERS

Fasting isn't just about feeling hungry; it's also about dealing with the emotional and mental challenges that pop up along the way. For many women over 50, the cognitive difficulties can feel just as daunting as the hunger itself. Worrying about missing out is a big hurdle for many. Just thinking about skipping your regular meals can freak you out, turning fasting into a punishment instead of a choice. This fear usually comes from past dieting attempts, where feeling deprived just didn't work out.

Additionally, there's the stress of attending social eating events. Feeling the pressure to fit in and enjoy group meals can be overwhelming. You may be concerned about how to explain your fasting lifestyle to friends and family who simply don't understand it.

Navigating these emotional hurdles requires building a positive mindset. Easy but impactful affirmations can change your mindset from feeling scarce to feeling abundant. Remind yourself regularly why you decided to fast, whether it's for improved health, increased energy, or enhanced mental clarity. It helps you stay committed to your goals. Being part of supportive communities or accountability groups can make a significant difference. These communities are all about sharing experiences, celebrating wins, and getting advice when things get tough. Realizing others are on the same journey can boost your spirits and make you feel less alone.

Self-awareness is the primary driving force in overcoming challenges. Keeping a diary is an excellent way to document your past successes and mental growth. By identifying your thoughts and feelings, you will discover the patterns and triggers that influence your fasting experience. Meditation can also significantly boost your mental resilience. Investing a few minutes daily in mindfulness can dramatically enhance your awareness of your thoughts and emotions, enabling you to respond to them with greater clarity and calm. This practice allows you to remain calm, even when social pressures or distractions attempt to upset you.

Check out Susan's story; she initially struggled with the social aspect of fasting. She was nervous about going to dinners and parties, dreading the need to explain her choices. Susan discovered the power of being present when she joined a mindfulness group. She began using meditation techniques to focus on the joy of the event rather than the food.

This change enabled her to dive into social events without fear or anxiety. Jane, a woman over 50, discovered that journaling was her secret weapon against the fear of failure. Jane boosted her self-confidence by tracking her little wins and reflecting on her journey, which fueled her success with fasting.

Emotional resilience is key to nailing your fasting goals. Tackle those mental blocks with care and purpose, and you'll make your fasting journey way more rewarding. As you continue on this journey, don't forget that the skills you develop, such as mindfulness, community, and self-awareness, will support your fasting goals and enhance your life even further.

11

LONG-TERM SUCCESS AND LIFESTYLE INTEGRATION

Imagine your body as a classic car in a quiet garage. It doesn't run all the time, but with regular tune-ups, a little polish, and some rest, it hums like new. Intermittent fasting works the same way. By providing your body space between meals, you're not depriving it; you're maintaining it. Every mindful choice is like checking the oil or tightening a bolt. Over time, that care adds up, and your body starts to run smoother, look better, and go the distance.

Keeping track of your fasting patterns is crucial to staying motivated and informed. Using your journals and apps to track your eating windows, reflect on your experiences, and identify any health improvements, both physical and mental, will provide you with a wealth of information that you can use to maximize your progress. For even more insight, keep track of how energized you feel throughout the day and note any mood shifts that occur. It'll give you a clear view of your fasting journey.

There are plenty of ways to measure success. Keeping an eye on your body measurements and weight is a straightforward way to monitor changes over time. Pay attention to how your clothes fit and how your energy levels change. Don't forget to monitor your mood swings; they can reveal just as much as your physical stats.

Setting goals that are actually achievable keeps you focused and motivated. Begin by setting short-term goals, such as adhering to a specific fasting schedule for a week. Hitting those smaller milestones gives you a boost and keeps you motivated to push forward. Long-term goals may include maintaining a healthy weight, boosting energy levels, or improving cognitive abilities. When you lay out your goals, you create a clear path that helps you stay focused and track your progress. Regularly checking in on your goals ensures they still align with your needs as things change. Feel free to tweak them as you learn more about what works for you with fasting.

It's important to celebrate your wins, big or small—every milestone you hit shows just how dedicated and hard you've been working. Whether you've lost pounds, gained more energy, or nailed your fasting plan for a month, give yourself a shoutout for those wins. They boost your confidence and drive, pushing you to keep moving ahead. It's not about where you are; it's about enjoying the journey and all the interesting stuff you learn along the way.

REFLECTION: SETTING GOALS AND TRACKING PROGRESS

Think about your fasting journey up to now. What goals have you knocked out? What new ones are you thinking of setting? Why not jot down your thoughts and experiences in a journal? It could be a game-changer! This practice helps you track your progress and provides a space for self-reflection and inspiration. Your journal is like a buddy, giving you the boost and perspective you need to keep pushing ahead with confidence and clarity.

EMBRACING AGING: FASTING FOR LONGEVITY

Picture your body like a strong oak tree, with deep roots in the ground and branches reaching up to the sky. This amazing tree grows in harmony with nature, just like our bodies do when we try intermittent fasting. This diet is key for healthy aging, kickstarting cellular repair and regeneration. When we fast, our bodies enter autophagy mode, much like an internal cleanup crew getting to work. It carefully removes damaged cells, making room for fresh, healthy ones to grow. This "cellular detox" helps reduce age-related inflammation linked to many chronic issues. Intermittent fasting allows our bodies to recharge, boosting our energy and resilience, just like an oak tree gets stronger through the seasons.

As we age, maintaining a healthy heart is crucial. Intermittent fasting can boost your heart health by lowering blood pressure and cholesterol levels. It boosts your brainpower, keeping your memory sharp and your mind resilient. Fasting increases your brain by ramping up the production of brain-derived neurotrophic factor (BDNF). This protein helps nerve cells grow and function more effectively. You may start remembering things better, feeling sharper mentally, and even help ward off age-related brain decline.

Incorporating mindfulness into your routine will help to fully maximize the benefits of fasting for longevity. Meditation, gentle yoga, or tai chi can significantly enhance your fasting experience by allowing you to relax and reduce stress. These practices help regulate stress hormones, such as cortisol, which is beneficial for both your mental and physical well-being.

Make sure to load up on nutrient-packed foods when you eat. Mix in a variety of colorful fruits and vegetables, lean proteins, and healthy fats to give your body the vitamins and minerals it needs to thrive. Every meal is an opportunity to nourish your body and lay the groundwork for a healthier future.

Longevity experts, especially gerontologists, often highlight how fasting could help you live longer. Studies have shown that fasting can impact nutrient-sensing pathways, such as the mTOR and IGF-1 pathways, which are associated with aging and longevity. Fasting could boost lifespan and enhance the time we spend feeling good by tweaking these pathways. It's all about maintaining a balanced lifestyle, staying active, and consuming whole foods. Fasting can really boost your energy and overall quality of life, paving the way for a lively and fulfilling future.

MAINTAINING MOTIVATION: TIPS FOR LONG-TERM COMMITMENT

Imagine the road ahead as a twisty path with milestones, each one showing how far you've come. Sometimes, motivation feels like a flickering flame, especially when you hit a plateau or get distracted by social gatherings with all those tempting treats. It can be tough when it feels like you're not making any headway, especially when you're the one at a party nursing a glass of water while everyone else is diving into those fancy snacks. Just keep in mind that these moments are all part of the journey. Seeing them as temporary keeps you focused on the bigger picture. Staying committed means you've been flexible, rolling with the ups and downs of the journey.

One way to stay motivated is by placing visual reminders around your home, such as sticky notes with positive affirmations on your mirror or a motivational quote on the fridge, to keep your motivation going. These little prompts are excellent reminders of why you got started in the first place.

Reflect, Celebrate, and Stay Accountable

Set aside some time each week for self-reflection to check in on your progress and remind yourself of your goals. This practice demonstrates your commitment and allows you to adjust your approach as needed. Celebrate every little win. They can really boost your motivation and keep you going strong.

Staying accountable is crucial to maintaining high motivation. Joining an online fasting group or teaming up with a friend who shares your health goals can really spice up your journey. It's fun to share your experiences with others. Partners and groups are there to back you up and lift your spirits, bringing fresh ideas and perspectives when you're low on motivation. A quick chat with a friend can spark your excitement and remind you that you're in this together. Discussing your ups and downs fosters a sense of community and support that helps you move forward.

Words of wisdom can really lift you up, especially when times get tough.

"Fasting isn't about deprivation. It's about making space, physically, mentally, and emotionally, for healing and clarity."
"When you stop feeding your distractions, you start feeding your purpose."
"In the stillness between meals, you meet the strongest version of yourself."
"True nourishment begins in the pause, not the plate."

These affirmations highlight the importance of perseverance and remind us that every day presents a new opportunity to move forward. Use these quotes as your go-to mantras to help you move through doubt and enjoy the process.

CONTINUING EDUCATION: RESOURCES FOR ONGOING SUPPORT

Consider your knowledge of intermittent fasting as a toolkit, one that becomes refined with every experience, enabling you to achieve long-term success. Being current, we continue to keep this toolkit oiled and operational. Stay informed about the latest studies to fine-tune your fasting strategies based on the most current information available. Bouncing other points of view off one another can really help to advance your knowledge and initiate fresh ideas and resolutions that might not have occurred to you otherwise.

Trusted Resources to Deepen Your Fasting Journey

To guide you on this path, consider a curated list of resources. Books like "The Complete Guide to Fasting" by Dr. Jason Fung offer in-depth knowledge and practical advice. Websites such as Healthline and the National Institute on Aging provide reliable health information and updates on fasting research. Podcasts like "The Intermittent Fasting Podcast" feature engaging discussions and expert interviews that can deepen your understanding of the topic. Or visit my doctor, Dr. Khan, at The Kahn Center for Cardiac Longevity, which features blogs, podcasts, and integrative medicine. Tuning into these resources can feel like sitting down with a knowledgeable friend, offering you new insights and sparking inspiration. They serve as companions on your journey, encouraging you to explore and learn at your own pace.

Fuel Your Fasting Knowledge Through Seminars and Workshops

Attending seminars and workshops is a wonderful opportunity to learn more and expand your horizons. Such conferences are filled with valuable information and provide a good opportunity to meet like-minded individuals. Discussing with other individuals who fast is an excellent way to enjoy a fine exchange of ideas and experiences. More-over, tips from the professionals might clear up any questions or confusion you have. Going to these events can spark your passion and commitment. There's something unique about spending time with individuals who share the same goals as you; that's inspiring and motivational.

Separating Fasting Facts from Fiction

In today's digital age, finding credible information can be challenging. Much of the information posted online is not evidence-based, so it is worthwhile to seek credible sources. Discerning crucial content is key to making informed decisions. Check the credentials of authors and experts to ensure their advice is rooted in science and expertise. Reliable sources often cite their references, allowing you to verify the information against reputable research. Applying this critical eye can build a library of trustworthy resources, enhancing your knowledge and empowering your fasting practice. When seeking information about fasting, ask a few questions:

1. Who is the author, and what are their qualifications?

2. Are there research studies or expert opinions that support the formation provided?

3. Are the claims exaggerated?

Use information from reputable health organizations or peer-reviewed journals for accurate and reliable sources. Healthcare professionals can provide information tailored to your health issues. Knowledgeable choices empower you to make informed decisions that align with your health goals and lifestyle. Trust that your critical thinking skills can discern fact from fiction, taking you to a healthier, happier life.

INSPIRING SUCCESS STORIES: WOMEN OVER 50 WHO THRIVED

Lina, age 57, felt constantly tired and struggled to lose the stubborn extra pounds. She jumped into intermittent fasting with a straightforward 16:8 plan. In just a few months, Lina noticed her waistline shrinking and felt more energized than ever. She was buzzing with energy and finally felt like she had her health back on track after years of struggle. Lina's journey demonstrates the renewing power of fasting, offering hope and encouragement to anyone who is contemplating this life-altering transformation.

Maria was coping with mood swings and frustrating brain fog that so often accompanies menopause. At 62, Maria started fasting to shake off the mental fog. She began to notice a significant improvement in her mental clarity and emotional stability over time. Maria says that fasting helped her boost her confidence and resilience, enabling her to tackle each day with a clear mind and a positive attitude. Her story demonstrates that fasting isn't just about physical health; it also significantly enhances mental and emotional wellness.

Every woman is unique and is motivated by her own set of health goals and experiences. Meet Joan, who had been battling high blood pressure for years. Joan combined fasting with a healthy diet, and it was pure magic; her blood pressure stabilized, and she felt so much more in control of her health. Her story demonstrates how fasting can be tailored to address specific health issues and how it can be adjusted to meet individual needs. These women's experiences remind us that patience and persistence do matter. Fasting is not an overnight fix; it is a way of life that demands commitment and some compromise.

Community support was a game-changer in all these stories. These women found support and motivation from others on similar journeys, whether in online forums or local groups. Feeling like you belong and sharing a goal can be super powerful, giving you the boost to tackle tough times. Journaling or sharing your experiences can be a powerful way to inspire yourself and stay accountable. Let these stories inspire you to reflect on your fasting journey, see how far you've come, and celebrate every win along the way.

YOUR JOURNEY AHEAD: EMBRACING A HEALTHIER FUTURE

Imagine the road ahead as a lively mix of health and energy, bursting with color. Imagine a future where intermittent fasting is an integral part of your everyday routine, enhancing your health and leaving you feeling great. Setting new health and wellness goals is an exciting prospect. If you're looking to boost your energy, lift your mood, or maintain a healthy weight, these goals can significantly shape your daily decisions. Making fasting a part of your everyday life means fitting it into your routine so it helps you navigate life's ups and downs with ease and strength.

Intermittent fasting isn't just about when you eat; it's about **intention**. It invites you to step off the rollercoaster of constant consumption and into a space of clarity, awareness, and control. When practiced mindfully, fasting becomes more than a wellness strategy; it becomes a path to **self-actualization**.

Just as self-actualization is the process of becoming the highest version of yourself, one that is aligned, empowered, and purposeful. Fasting strips away what's unnecessary. It teaches you to sit with discomfort, trust your body's wisdom, and reconnect with the quiet strength that's always been there. You learn to ask more profound questions:

- Am I hungry or just distracted?
- Am I eating out of habit or emotion?
- What would nourish me more deeply, food or stillness?

Fasting not only strengthens your metabolism but also enhances your **mental resilience, emotional intelligence,** and **spiritual discipline**. It shifts your focus from momentary cravings to long-term transformation. It encourages delayed gratification, a hallmark of self-mastery, and creates space for you to listen to your body, intuition, and life.

In this way, intermittent fasting becomes a daily practice of self-discovery and transformation.

A pause that reawakens purpose.

A reset that reveals potential.

*A ritual that supports the journey, not just to a healthier body, but to your most **actualized self**.*

CONCLUSION

As we conclude our journey, let's take a quick moment to reflect on the purpose and vision that guided us through these pages. I wanted to inspire you, as a woman over 50, by highlighting the transformative power of intermittent fasting. Demonstrate how this lifestyle can boost your energy, balance hormones, help with weight management, and keep your mind sharp. I hope the tips and tricks in this book have fired you up to use fasting as a way to boost your energy and health.

Alright, let's go over the main points we've talked about. We kicked things off with the basics of intermittent fasting, exploring its benefits and how it differs for women over 50. We delved into the hormonal health benefits, discussing how fasting can support you during menopause and beyond. We explored weight management, mental wellness, and bone health, providing a well-rounded perspective on how fasting impacts our bodies. We explored how to effectively implement strategies, incorporate exercise, and address the social and emotional aspects of fasting. We addressed common challenges and laid the groundwork for long-term success.

CONCLUSION

This book highlights the importance of personalized fasting plans, holistic health practices, community support, self-awareness, and adaptability. Here are the key points to keep in mind. Your fasting journey is unique, so be sure to tailor it to fit your specific needs and lifestyle. Take a well-rounded approach and feed your body, mind, and soul. Find your tribe and don't be shy about asking for support and learning together. Stay attuned to your own experiences and be prepared to adjust as you evolve.

Intermittent fasting has been a truly eye-opening experience that has changed my life for the better. It's pumped me up with fresh energy, clear thinking, and a solid grip on my health. Fasting has significantly enhanced my emotional resilience and self-confidence. By sharing my journey, I hope you can also reap these benefits.

As you begin your fasting journey, remember that the emotional and mental benefits are just as significant as the physical ones. Fasting is all about taking care of yourself and showing yourself some love. It's all about respecting your body and prioritizing your health. When you start fasting, you'll notice some changes right away: standing taller, feeling more confident, and just glowing with energy.

Why not take that first step today? You got this! Take it easy and give yourself some time to grow. Check out the tools and resources in this book to help you out. Just a reminder: every journey kicks off with that first step. Believe in the journey and have faith in yourself. You can change your health and life one day at a time.

Feel free to share your stories and connect with others who are on the same journey. Join online groups, attend workshops, or simply chat with friends and family. Strength comes from numbers, and by sharing your story, you may just inspire someone else to embark on their own journey.

CONCLUSION

Thank you for being part of this journey! I really appreciate your trust, dedication, and willingness to try something new.

With gratitude and encouragement, Claudia Von.

END OF BOOK REVIEW

Keeping the Game Alive

Now that you've learned how intermittent fasting can help you feel stronger, healthier, and more energized after 50, it's time to pass on that gift of knowledge to others.

By leaving your honest opinion of this book on Amazon, you'll show other women over 50 exactly where they can find the tools and encouragement they need to begin their own journey.

Think of it as lighting the path for someone who's just a few steps behind you. Your words can give her the courage to start, the clarity to keep going, and the hope that lasting change is possible.

Thank you for being part of this movement. Intermittent fasting for women over 50 stays alive when we share what we know—and you're helping me do just that.

<u>Click here to leave your review on Amazon</u>

Or Click on the QR code below.

With heartfelt thanks,

Claudia Von

INTERMITTENT FASTING SCHEDULE QUESTIONNAIRE

1. What is your primary goal for intermittent fasting?

· A. Weight loss and fat burning

· B. Improved energy and mental clarity

· C. Support overall health and longevity

· D. Balance hormones and ease into fasting gently

2. How experienced are you with fasting?

· A. I'm a complete beginner.

· B. I've tried short fasting windows (skipping a meal).

· C. I've successfully done longer fasts (16+ hours).

· D. I'm comfortable with extended or challenging fasting protocols.

3. What is your current eating pattern?

· A. I often skip breakfast or dinner.

· B. I eat three regular meals a day.

· C. My eating schedule varies day to day.

· D. I tend to graze or snack throughout the day.

4. How important is flexibility in your schedule?

· A. I need a plan that fits into my daily routine with minimal change.

· B. I can manage some structured eating windows.

· C. I'm okay with having "normal" eating days and strict fasting days.

· D. I want to challenge myself with a disciplined structure.

5. What is your activity level?

· A. Low to moderate (casual walks, light exercise).

· B. Moderate to high (regular workouts, active job).

· C. Very high (intense training, athletic goals).

· D. Varies day-to-day.

6. What time of day do you feel most energetic?

· A. Morning

· B. Afternoon

· C. Evening

· D. It fluctuates day-to-day

7. Are you trying to maintain muscle while losing fat?

· A. Yes, that's one of my top priorities.

· B. Somewhat, but my main goal is fat loss.

· C. Not a big concern for me right now.

8. Do you struggle with cravings late at night or in the morning?

- A. Late at night

- B. In the morning

- C. Both

- D. Neither

9. Do you have any existing health conditions (hypoglycemia, thyroid, hormone imbalance, etc.)?

- A. Yes, and I need a gentle approach.

- B. No, I'm generally healthy.

- C. I have some conditions, but my doctor has cleared me for fasting.

- D. I'm not sure, I'd start cautiously.

10. How many days per week can you realistically commit to fasting?

- A. Daily (consistent routine works best for me).

- B. 3–5 days a week.

- C. Only a couple of days per week.

- D. I prefer an every-other-day structure.

———

Answer Key

Mostly A's. 14:10 or 12:12

- Best for beginners, hormone balance, or those easing into fasting. Gentle approach that supports steady energy and sustainable habits.

Mostly B's. 16:8

· Great for weight loss, metabolic health, and mental clarity. Works well if you naturally skip a meal and prefer consistency.

Mostly C's. 5:2

· Perfect for those wanting flexibility while still losing weight and improving health. Eat normally 5 days a week, fast or eat very low-calorie (500–600) for 2 days.

Mostly D's. Alternate-Day Fasting (ADF)

· Suited for experienced fasters, disciplined individuals, or those seeking rapid metabolic improvements. Eat normally one day, fast or eat very low-calorie the next.

BONUS CHAPTER

Click on the QR Code below for recipes, weekly meal plans, weekly exercise routines, and much more!

REFERENCES

- *WebMD. (n.d.). Intermittent fasting for women over 50: What you need to know. WebMD. https://www.webmd.com/healthy-aging/what-to-know-about-intermittent-fasting-for-women-after-50#:~:?text=For%20-women%20over%2050%2C%20intermit-tent,you%20try%20this%20eating%20plan*

- *Gunnars, K. (2023, June 28). 16/8 intermittent fasting: Meal plan, benefits, and more. Healthline. https://www.healthline.com/nutrition/16-8-intermittent-fasting*

- *Brighten, J. (n.d.). Intermittent fasting for menopause: What you need to know. Dr. Jolene Brighten. https://drbrighten.com/intermittent-fasting-for-menopause/#:~:text=Intermittent%20fasting%20during%20menopause%20-can,also%20reducing%20certain%20menopausal%20symptoms*

- *Ware, M. (2023, September 25). The definitive guide to healthy eating in your 50s and 60s. Healthline. https://www.healthline.com/nutrition/healthy-eating-50s-60s*

- *Johns Hopkins Medicine. (n.d.). Introduction to menopause. Johns Hopkins Medicine. https://www.hopkinsmedicine.org/health/conditions-and-diseases/introduction-to-menopause#:~:text=During%20this%20transition%20-time%20before,of%20the%20symptoms%20of%20menopause*

- *Liu, Y., Cheng, J., & Wang, Y. (2021). Effects of intermittent fasting on the circulating levels and circadian rhythms of metabolic biomarkers. Frontiers in Nutrition, 8, 709402. https://doi.org/10.3389/fnut.2021.709402*

- *WebMD. (n.d.). The best ways to increase metabolism after 50. WebMD. https://www.webmd.com/healthy-aging/increasing-metabolism-after-50*

- *Medical News Today. (2023, April 27). 10 evidence-based health benefits of intermittent fasting. Medical News Today. https://www.medicalnewstoday.com/articles/323605*

- *Anton, S. (n.d.). How to break out of an intermittent fasting plateau. Dr. Stephen Anton. https://drstephenanton.com/intermittent-fasting-plateau/*

- *University of California San Diego. (2021, September 28). Study: Time-restricted eating may improve health of adults with metabolic syndrome. UC San Diego Today. https://today.ucsd.edu/story/study-time-restricted-eating-may-improve-health-of-adults-with-metabolic-syndrome*

- *Rogers, P. J., & Appleton, K. M. (2021). Intermittent fasting and cognitive performance. Nutrition Research, 87, 1–12. https://doi.org/10.1016/j.nutres.2021.01.003*

- Adams, R. (2024, September 16). *4 surprising emotional benefits of intermittent fasting.* Psychology Today. https://www.psychologytoday.com/us/blog/liking-the-child-you-love/202409/4-surprising-emotional-benefits-of-intermittent-fasting

- Bone health: Tips to keep your bones healthy. (2023, September 1). Mayo Clinic. https://www.mayoclinic.org/healthy-lifestyle/adult-health/in-depth/bone-health/art-20045060

- Calcium and vitamin D: Important for bone health. (2022, March). National Institute of Arthritis and Musculoskeletal and Skin Diseases. https://www.niams.nih.gov/health-topics/calcium-and-vitamin-d-important-bone-health

- Cryan, J. F., & Dinan, T. G. (2019). The gut-brain axis: Influence of microbiota on mood and behavior. *Clinical Practice, 12*(2), 59–73. https://pmc.ncbi.nlm.nih.gov/articles/PMC6469458/

- Fasting for gut health: Benefits and how-tos. (2023, May 22). *Health.* https://www.health.com/nutrition/how-to-fast-healthy-gut

- Intermittent fasting: What is it, and how does it work? (n.d.). Johns Hopkins Medicine. https://www.hopkinsmedicine.org/health/wellness-and-prevention/intermittent-fasting-what-is-it-and-how-does-it-work

- Li, G., Xie, C., Lu, S., Nichols, R. G., Tian, Y., Li, L., Patel, D., Ma, Y., Brocker, C. N., Yan, T., Krausz, K. W., Xiang, R., Gavrilova, O., Patterson, A. D., & Gonzalez, F. J. (2023). Intermittent fasting reduces neuroinflammation and improves behavior in mice. *Frontiers in Immunology, 14,* 1162290. https://pmc.ncbi.nlm.nih.gov/articles/PMC10780385/

- Maifeld, A., Bartolomaeus, H., & Wilck, N. (2024). The impact of intermittent fasting on gut microbiota. *Nutrients, 16*(2), 321. https://pmc.ncbi.nlm.nih.gov/articles/PMC10894978/

- Moro, T., & Paoli, A. (2021). Intermittent fasting and sleep: A review of human trials. *Nutrients, 13*(10), 3479. https://pubmed.ncbi.nlm.nih.gov/34684490/

- Nutrium. (2023, January 15). *Bone health and nutrition: Meal plans for clients with osteoporosis.* Nutrium. https://nutrium.com/blog/bone-health-and-nutrition-meal-plans-for-clients-with-osteoporosis/

- News-Medical. (2023, August 18). *The effect of intermittent fasting on the gut microbiome.* News-Medical.net. https://www.news-medical.net/health/The-Effect-of-Intermittent-Fasting-on-the-Gut-Microbiome.aspx#:~:text=Recent%20studies%20suggest%20that%20intermittent,anaerobic%20bacteria%20called%20Lachnospiraceae%20flourished

REFERENCES

- Berkeley, L. (2023, April 3). *10 best intermittent fasting apps for weight loss.* Good Housekeeping. https://www.goodhousekeeping.com/health-products/g34618367/best-apps-intermittent-fasting/

- Carter, K. (2024, March 22). *Yoga over 50: 14 yoga poses that you can do at any age.* Lots of Yoga. https://lotsofyoga.com/blogs/yoga-tips/yoga-over-50-best-yoga-poses

- Medical News Today. (2023, August 9). *Intermittent fasting and exercise: How to do it safely.* Medical News Today. https://www.medicalnewstoday.com/articles/intermittent-fasting-and-working-out

- Prevention Editors. (2023, March 28). *Intermittent fasting for women over 50: What to know.* Prevention. https://www.prevention.com/weight-loss/diets/a61413679/intermittent-fasting-women-over-50/

- Skerrett, P. (2023, February 20). *Exercise tips for women over 50.* WebMD. https://www.webmd.com/women/women-over-50-fitness-tips

- U.S. News & World Report. (2024, January 15). *Intermittent fasting recipes and meal plans.* U.S. News & World Report. https://health.us-news.com/best-diet/intermittent-fasting/recipe

- Walsh, J. (2024, May 12). *Strength training is a must for women in midlife — Here's why.* The Flow Space. https://www.theflowspace.com/physical-health/prevention-longevity/strength-training-women-over-50-2938818/

- 12 Oaks Senior Living. (2023, April 5). *Intermittent fasting for seniors: Benefits & safety guide.* 12 Oaks Senior Living. https://12oak-s.net/intermittent-fasting-for-seniors/

- Azevedo, R. (2024, January 19). *Intermittent fasting for women over 50.* Mindbodygreen. https://www.mindbodygreen.com/articles/intermittent-fasting-for-women-over-50?srsltid=AfmBOorHWQWfyDADXm_h-Lq3_1XYBagxdijHIp-IPXvoWiqoULaxLuJlM

- Berkeley, L. (2023, April 3). *10 best intermittent fasting apps for weight loss.* Good Housekeeping. https://www.goodhousekeeping.com/health-products/g34618367/best-apps-intermittent-fasting/

- Catterson, J. H., & Partridge, L. (2022). Intermittent and periodic fasting, longevity, and disease. *Nature Aging, 2*(5), 447–458. https://pmc.ncbi.nlm.nih.gov/articles/PMC8932957/

- Dawn Health. (2023, November 14). *The power of fasting: Positive impacts for kids and parents.* Dawn Health. https://www.dawnhealth.care/blog/the-power-of-fasting-positive-impacts-for-kids-and-parents

- Horne, B. D., Grajower, M. M., & Anderson, J. L. (2015). Fasting: Molecular mechanisms and clinical applications. *Cell Metabolism, 19*(2), 181–192. https://www.sciencedirect.com/science/article/pii/S1550413113005032

REFERENCES

- Lifesum. (2023, July 6). *How to navigate social situations while fasting.* Lifesum. https://lifesum.com/nutrition-explained/how-to-navigate-social-situations-while-fasting

- Meetup. (n.d.). *Intermittent fasting groups.* Meetup. https://www.meetup.com/topics/intermittent-fasting/

- SlimFast. (n.d.). *Managing hunger while intermittent fasting.* SlimFast. https://slimfast.com/intermittent-fasting/managing-hunger-while-intermittent-fasting/

- Zero Longevity Science. (2023, February 10). *8 fasting myths, debunked.* Zero Longevity Science. https://zerolongevity.com/blog/8-fasting-myths-debunked/#:~:text=Fasting%20Myth%20%234%3A%20Fasting%20Slows%20Down%20Your%20Metabolism&text=But%20that%20s%20wrong!,timing%20play%20a%20larger%20role

- Zero Longevity Science. (2023, May 18). *How to pair mindful eating with mindful fasting.* Zero Longevity Science. https://zerolongevity.com/blog/how-to-pair-mindful-eating-with-mindful-fasting/

- Intermittent Fasting Success Story: Fasting After Menopause https://usetemper.com/learn/intermittent-fasting-success-story-fasting-after-menopause/?srsltid=AfmBOopBXRfrnTma-tWt4nOuksBHncoEDabr9ZxWFWVzvhbBPw-Y9GBm

- Dykstra, B., Hidde, M., Erichsen, J., & Mahon, A. D. (2017). Metabolic Flexibility In Lean Children. Medicine and Science in Sports and Exercise. https://doi.org/10.1249/01.mss.0000518081.80513.00

- Boosting Metabolism in Midlife: Strategies for Revitalizing Your Body. https://www.midlifehealthcoach.com/blog/metabolism

- Loss of muscle mass - Hormone Harmony Clinic. https://testosteronecost.com/glossary/loss-of-muscle-mass/

- Menopause Symptom: Weight Gain. https://goldenleafhc.com/menopause/weight-gain/

- CBD: The Unexpected Ally Against Alzheimer's Disease. https://www.corney-barrow.co.uk/cbd-alzheimers-disease-potential-treatment/

- The Benefits Of Fasting. https://blog.ijugaad.com/the-benefits-of-fasting/

- How to Stop Emotional Eating Without Feeling Deprived | simongPT. https://www.simongpt.co.uk/how-to-stop-emotional-eating-without-feeling-deprived/

- Mindfulness for Breaking Bad Habits - Body & Mind Online. https://bodymindonline.com.au/mindfulness-for-bad-habits/

- Hippocampal Volume Loss in Alzheimer's Disease – HelpDementia.com. https://helpdementia.com/hippocampal-volume-loss-in-alzheimers-disease/

REFERENCES

- Unlocking Your Brain's Full Potential: A Guide to Enhancing Cognitive Function - System Ent Corp. https://systementcorp.com/unlocking-your-brain ' https://systementcorp.com/unlocking-your-brains-full-potential-a-guide-to-enhancing-cognitive-function/
- Sleeping Better with Yoga and Meditation | Fit On. https://fit-on.net/sleeping-better-with-yoga-and-meditation/
- Understand Circadian Rhythm: Sync Your Life for Better Sleep. https://sleepingsavvy.com/understanding-the-circadian-rhythm/
- The Benefits Of Fasting. https://blog.ijugaad.com/the-benefits-of-fasting/
- Hunger Games: Body vs. Emotions - Winning the Fight Against Emotional Eating. https://www.amyenglishcc.com/post/hunger-games-body-vs-emotions-winning-the-fight-against-emotional-eating
- Understanding Your Sleep Study Results. https://bcoh.com/understanding-your-sleep-study-results/
- Unlocking Your Brain's Full Potential: A Guide to Enhancing Cognitive Function - System Ent Corp. https://systementcorp.com/unlocking-your-brain ' https://systementcorp.com/unlocking-your-brains-full-potential-a-guide-to-enhancing-cognitive-function/
- Beyond the Myth: Discovering Your Active Sleep Potential - The Alchemy Of Being. https://thealchemyofbeing.me/beyond-the-myth-discovering-your-active-sleep-potential/
- Bone Up on Bone Disease - alive magazine. https://www.alive.com/health/bone-up-on-bone-disease/
- 8 Myths & Misconceptions Of Vitamin D Debunked - Love4wellness. https://love4wellness.com/vitamin-d-myths-misconceptions-debunked/
- How to Make Savory Slow-Cooked Lamb with Flavorful Lentils. https://recipesforbaking.com/recipes/slow-cooked-lamb-with-flavorful-lentils/
- The Top 10 Benefits of Protein Powder – Frontrow. https://luxxewhiteproducts.com/en-jp/blogs/news/the-top-10-benefits-of-protein-powder
- 5 Intermittent Fasting Tips for Weight Loss. https://www.fortodaysagingwoman.com/blog/unlocking-the-secret-to-weight-loss-for-women-over-50-with-intermittent-fasting-5-must-try-tips
- 10 Healthy Lunch Ideas To Fuel Your Day! Quick And Easy.. https://dishheaven.com/10-healthy-lunch-ideas-to-fuel-your-day/
- Hydration Solutions. https://backpackequipment.curatedspot.com/resources/hydration-solutions
- How to Combine Intermittent Fasting with Exercise for Maximum Fat Loss - Vitality Weight Loss Institute. https://vitalityweightlossinstitute.com/

dieting/how-to-combine-intermittent-fasting-with-exercise-for-maximum-fat-loss/

- Top 5 Health Benefits of Fibre - Dr. Swati Attam. https://www.drswatiattam.com/web-stories/health-benefits-of-fibre/
- Why Do Supergreens Support Healthy Digestive Function? – Nummies. https://getnummies.com/blogs/articles/why-do-supergreens-support-healthy-digestive-function
- Gut-Friendly Foods for a Healthy Digestive System. https://civilizedcaveman.com/health/gut-friendly-foods-digestive-health/
- Gut-Friendly Foods for a Healthy Digestive System. https://civilizedcaveman.com/health/gut-friendly-foods-digestive-health/
- Empowering Your Health: Nutrition Strategies for Managing Diabetes - My Health Concierge. https://www.myconciergehealth.org/2023/12/12/empowering-your-health-nutrition-strategies-for-managing-diabetes/
- Pinterest 08192024-1 – Daily Nutritional Blog. https://dailynutritionalblog.com/pinterest-08192024-1/
- Apple and Cranberry Overnight Oats. https://www.syrnyk.xyz/uk/blog/d41f81b6-c249-4703-9ea5-7cfd8b3ca7d6
- Lettuce Avocado Salad - What's for Dinner Today? https://whatsfordinnertoday.com/avocado-salad/
- 35+ High-Protein Dinners That Feel Like a Treat – jafifs.com. https://jafifs.com/35-high-protein-dinners/
- Garlic Chicken Stir-Fry | DEESVIRAL. https://deesviral.com/garlic-chicken-stir-fry/
- Hobbies and Activities for Seniors at Home: Stay Active and Engaged - Fort Worth Seniors. https://fortworthseniors.com/hobbies-and-activities-for-seniors-at-home-stay-active-and-engaged/
- The Importance of Regular Exercise - fknservices.com. https://fknservices.com/the-importance-of-regular-exercise-2/
- Why Strength Training is Important - What You Need to Know – MAXPRO Fitness. https://maxprofitness.com/blogs/news/why-strength-training-is-important
- The Intermittent Fasting and Strength Training Combo: A Match Made in Muscle-Building Heaven? - stack. https://www.stack.com/a/the-intermittent-fasting-and-strength-training-combo-a-match-made-in-muscle-building-heaven/page/3/
- Stay Safe: Workout Injury Tips | LifeSmart+. https://www.lifesmart.dev/workout-injury-tips

REFERENCES

- Cardio versus Strength Training. https://nihalatsiz.org/cardio-versus-strength-training-which-is-best-for-you/
- Transformative Yoga Sessions in Luxembourg or Online. https://noandme-yoga.com/services/yoga
- The Art of Mindful Eating: Strategies for a Healthy Relationship with Food - Dr. Chetan Kalal - drchetankalal. https://drchetankalal.com/the-art-of-mindful-eating-strategies-for-a-healthy-relationship-with-food-dr-chetan-kalal/
- Different Types of Hunger | Physical, Emotional, Sensory. https://withinhealth.com/learn/articles/types-of-hunger
- Is It Safe for Diabetics to Do Intermittent Fasting: Expert Insights. https://omojohealthusa.com/is-it-safe-for-diabetics-to-do-intermittent-fasting/
- Some Thoughts About Dealing With The Emotional And Mental Challenges Life Brings You. https://www.mitchhorton.com/post/some-thoughts-about-dealing-with-the-emotional-and-mental-challenges-life-brings-you
- #TheGOALdenList: Mindfulness Tips For Your Mental And Emotional Well-being | AIC Stories | Agency for Integrated Care. https://www.aic-blog.com/thegoaldenlist-mindfulness-tips-your-mental-and-emotional-well-being
- Unleash Your Potential: The Power of Accountability with a Life & Wellness Coach. https://www.lighthousecoachingus.com/post/unleash-your-potential-the-power-of-accountability-with-a-life-wellness-coach
- The Importance of Relationships and Social Connections: LYF Mail. https://lyfmail.com/self-help/importance-relationships-and-social-connections
- Benefits of intermittent fasting for health: Unlocking the Power of Fasting – Patient care. https://patiientcare.info/benefits-of-intermittent-fasting-for-health/
- https://recipesworthrepeating.com/naval-orange-and-kale-salad-2/?utm_source=chatgpt.com
- https://www.snapcalorie.com/recipes/heart-healthy_zesty_kale_salad_with_citrus_vinaigrette.html?utm_source=chatgpt.com

Printed in Dunstable, United Kingdom

71170198R00080